FEILDEN'S MERSEY

A selection of the post-war ship photographs of Basi

John Clarkson and Roy Fenton

Ships in Focus Publications

Published in the UK in 2001 by Ships in Focus Publications,18 Franklands, Longton, Preston PR4 5PD

Printed by Amadeus Press Ltd., Cleckheaton
ISBN 1 901703 61 4

Introduction

Basil Feilden was one of the most gifted photographers to have recorded the shipping scene on the Mersey during some of its most glorious years. Basil's work combined artistry with technical expertise: he had the perfect eye for a ship photograph, and almost invariably produced pin-sharp images which were beautifully lit. The postcards which he printed from his own negatives have long been prized by collectors.

This is the first major published collection of Basil's work, and covers the years after the war, from the time he resumed photography in 1950 to when he gave up after a vital piece of his camera was lost. For many years most of Basil's negatives have been in the collection of John Clarkson, who has made prints available. However, most of the negatives used here have recently been acquired from another collector who purchased them direct from Basil, and John has not previously printed from them.

The appeal of handsome ships photographed on the Mersey extends well beyond ship enthusiasts, and the captions in this book have been written to appeal both to a general audience curious to know about this or that ship and what it was doing in the Mersey, and to the more knowledgeable ship enthusiast. Details of builder, date, gross tonnage, length and engines for each ship are included.

The compilers hope that this selection will give pleasure to all who remember the Mersey and its ships in what was in many ways a golden age, and to those who would like to experience these years through some of the finest photographs ever taken on the river.

John Clarkson
Longton

Roy Fenton
Wimbledon

October 2001

Basil Feilden

Basil G.A. Feilden was born in 1908 near Bradford, moving with his parents to Blundellsands, Liverpool when he was a boy. Basil was first attracted to ships when he was taken by his father to the Mersey shore at Crosby on 30th May 1914 to see the *Aquitania* leaving for the first time. He later recalled the smell of smoke and the noise of the powerful siren.

There was no previous family interest in photography, but both Basil and his brother Alan became photographers, the latter with the RAF in India during the war. Basil was self-taught: starting with a Kodak Brownie, he moved first to a bigger Brownie and then to an Ensign folding camera which took postcard-sized negatives. Next came an Ensign de luxe reflex camera which he carried around strapped to the back of his motorcycle. It took 6½ by 4¾ inch negatives which gave plenty of scope for printing to postcard size. Basil did his own developing and printing in a darkroom at home.

Local newspapers were consulted for information on shipping movements and expected arrivals, and if photographing from the shore Basil would try to be on hand two hours before high water. He did not go aboard the vessels he photographed, but did have a tug pass. He would often go out in the tugs in all weathers, when holding the camera steady could be a problem. His working area was on both sides of the Mersey, up to Eastham. He travelled on foot and by 'bus and, from 1937, on his New Imperial 350cc motorcycle. When working, Basil would often alarm onlookers by walking backwards along a quay looking through his camera and feeling his way along the edge with his feet.

Basil made a living out of his photography, seeking customers by word of mouth and by placing advertisements in 'Meccano Magazine', 'Sea Breezes' and 'Ships and Ship Models'. The 'Journal of Commerce and Shipping Telegraph' used his photographs of new vessels. He also sold his postcards through bookshops and stationers such as Taylor's bookshop on the Liverpool landing stage.

After the war, during which Basil worked as an airframe fitter, he was able to resume his photography about 1950. He gave up around 1960. He lost the phosphor bronze mounting of his camera while attempting to stop a child falling into Gladstone Dock, Liverpool; and the camera finally broke when he was photographing the *Empress of Britain*. Basil died at Southport in December 1995.

Notes

Photographs are arranged in the approximate order of passenger and cargo liners, tramps, coasters and tankers, with British ships tending to come first. Details given for each, below the text, are: builder, date, tonnage in the 1950s, overall length in the first line; and in the second line type of engine and builder. Here Q. 4-cyl. is a quadruple-expansion four-cylinder steam engine, T. 3-cyl. is a triple-expansion three-cylinder steam engine, C. 2-cyl. is a compound two-cylinder steam engine. For oil engines, 2SC and 4SC are two-stroke and four-stroke cycle, SA is single-acting and DA double-acting.

EMPRESS OF AUSTRALIA (1)

When Basil Feilden resumed ship photography about 1950, there were still many reminders of the war on and around the Mersey. Here, he has photographed the *Empress of Australia*, not in the dazzling white livery for which Canadian Pacific was famous, but the drab and work-stained garb of a troopship. She wore these colours continuously from September 1939 until May 1952 when she left the Mersey to be broken up in Scotland.

She had been built for the Hamburg-Amerika Line as *Tirpitz*, but was not complete on the outbreak of war in 1914 and never sailed for Germany. Post-war reparations saw her come to Britain, and she was bought by Canadian Pacific who initially called her *Empress of China* but then thought better of it, and it was as *Empress of Australia* that she entered service on their trans-Pacific sailings.

Her original machinery was never satisfactory, and she was taken in hand on the Clyde in 1926 and fitted with Parson's turbines which increased her speed to 19 knots. In June 1927 she re-entered service on the Southampton to Quebec route on which she remained until the outbreak of the Second World War.

Vulkan Werke A.G., Stettin, Germany; 1913, 21,833gt, 590 feet
Six sets of steam turbines by Fairfield Shipbuilding and Engineering Co. Ltd., Govan driving twin screws

EMPRESS OF CANADA

This Empress started life as *Duchess of Richmond*, but rose in the ranks of royalty after her war service. She was requisitioned in February 1940 and sailed for over six years as a troopship without serious accident. On being demobbed in 1946, *Duchess of Richmond* was extensively refitted on the Clyde, and in July 1947 sailed from Liverpool on her maiden post-war voyage as *Empress of Canada*. As Basil Feilden's photograph above testifies, she was kept in superb external condition.

Alas, her peacetime career was not to be peaceful. On 25th January 1953 fire broke out whilst the *Empress of Canada* was lying in Gladstone Dock, and she subsequently capsized: note her bent funnel (right). After one of the biggest post-war salvage operations in Liverpool Docks, she was brought upright on 6th March, and on 1st September the burnt-out hulk - now anything but a 'White Empress' - left the Mersey under tow for breakers in Italy.

John Brown and Co. Ltd., Clydebank; 1928, 20,325gt, 582 feet
Six sets of steam turbines by John Brown and Co. Ltd., Clydebank driving twin screws

DE GRASSE and EMPRESS OF AUSTRALIA (2)

The loss of *Empress of Canada* left Canadian Pacific short of passenger ships, so in March 1953 they bought a rather elderly French lady, *De Grasse*, seen right arriving on the Mersey, which was renamed *Empress of Australia*. In coming to the Mersey she was returning to her birthplace. She had not been a happy experience for builders Cammell, Laird, as she was almost cancelled once, and a strike meant her owners, the French Line, took her off to be completed in France.

With the arrival of the new *Empress of Britain* in 1956, this *Empress of Australia* was sold to Italian owners and she swapped the North Atlantic for the South, sailing from the Mediterranean to Venezuela as *Venezuela*. In early 1962 she ran aground off Cannes, and after this mishap she was sold for scrap.

Cammell, Laird and Co. Ltd., Birkenhead; 1924, 17,707gt, 552 feet
Four steam turbines by Cammell, Laird and Co. Ltd., Birkenhead driving twin screws

SAMARIA

Cunard Line had risen to greatness as a Liverpool company, but then its largest and best liners deserted the Mersey for Southampton. Amongst the attractions of the southern port was its closeness to London, and the four tides a day which gave more options for sailings.

Occasionally, a Southampton-based Cunarder put in an appearance on the Mersey in post-war years, including the *Samaria*, an example of 1920s elegance. When new she ran from Liverpool to Boston but, after war service as a troopship, was refitted and during the 1950s ran mainly between Southampton and Quebec. She was broken up on the Forth in 1956.

Cammell, Laird and Co. Ltd., Birkenhead; 1921, 19,597gt, 602 feet
Six steam turbines by Cammell, Laird and Co. Ltd., Birkenhead driving twin screws

PARTHIA

A rump of Cunard passenger services was left at Liverpool, although with smaller and less impressive ships than their prestige express services. *Parthia*, which maintained Cunard's Liverpool to New York passenger sailings with her slightly older sister *Media*, were examples of cargo-passenger ships. They carried 250 first class passengers, and also had a large cargo capacity: note *Parthia's* many derricks. But, as passengers were discharged much quicker than cargo, whilst the ships were being laboriously unloaded their passenger accommodation was frequently idle, and with it the stewards that serviced it. By the 1960s, such ships had become uneconomic.

Cunard replaced the two sisters with pure cargo ships in 1961, and *Parthia* began a second career for the New Zealand Shipping Co. Ltd. as *Remuera*. But the same problems afflicted her on the New Zealand route, and she served for only two years. Her last days were spent running as *Aramac* in the Far East, where she was broken up in 1969.

Harland and Wolff Ltd., Belfast; 1948, 13,362gt, 531 feet
Four steam turbines by Harland and Wolff Ltd., Belfast driving twin screws

ARABIA

Like most liner companies, Cunard had a fleet of cargo carriers to complement their big passenger ships. In Cunard's case, their post-war cargo ships were a somewhat motley collection, with little in common except Cunard's well-known red funnel with black top and bands. Seen locking in to Liverpool's docks, *Arabia* with her sisters *Asia* and *Assyria* were amongst the first new ships built for the company after the war, and were intended to run both to New York and to Montreal.

In 1963 *Arabia* was sold to Japanese owners, who put her under the Liberian flag as *Onshun*. She was broken up in Taiwan during 1972.

Sir J. Laing and Sons Ltd., Sunderland; 1947, 8,720gt, 509 feet
Two steam turbines by Richardsons, Westgarth and Co. Ltd., Hartlepool driving a single screw

PAVIA

Whilst having the world's largest passenger liners, Cunard also had the miniature cargo liners *Pavia* and her sisters *Phrygia* and *Lycia* working on their routes to the Mediterranean. Their size reflected the need to enter a wide range of large and small ports, from Bari to Volo, Algiers to Varna. Cunard's sailing notices in the late 1950s listed 30 destinations.

Caught by Basil Feilden hurrying along the Mersey on a grey day, *Pavia's* career was cut short by containerisation and in 1965 she was sold to Greek owners as *Toula N.* She was broken up in Taiwan in 1974.

William Hamilton and Co. Ltd., Port Glasgow; 1953, 3,411gt, 384 feet
Four-cylinder 2SCSA Doxford-type oil engine by David Rowan and Co. Ltd., Glasgow

EMPIRE CLYDE

Anchor Line was based in Glasgow, but ships on both their North Atlantic and Indian routes were common sights in the Mersey, reflecting the importance of Liverpool.

Empire Clyde was built for Anchor Line as *Cameronia*, their first new ship for their North Atlantic service after the First World War. Her long career involved service as a troopship in the Second World War, when she was present at the invasions of North Africa, Sicily and Normandy. After the war she was laid up, apparently worn out, but in 1953 was reconditioned and, as *Empire Clyde*, carried troops and emigrants. Basil Feilden's photograph shows her in troopship colours of white hull with blue band and yellow funnel. Anchor Line continued to manage her until she was broken up in South Wales late in 1957.

William Beardmore and Co. Ltd., Dalmuir; 1920, 16,584gt, 575 feet
Six steam turbines by William Beardmore and Co. Ltd., Dalmuir driving twin screws

CALEDONIA

Anchor Line's naming scheme was very similar to Cunard's but this seems to have been a coincidence; Cunard did buy out the company in 1911, but the scheme was in place long before this date.

Seen about to enter Birkenhead, *Caledonia* was one of three diesel-engined passenger ships which maintained Anchor Line's sailings from Glasgow and Liverpool to Bombay, being a virtual repeat of the pre-war *Circassia* and *Cilicia*. All three were made redundant when the service ended in 1965, but *Caledonia* found sedentary employment as a student hostel in Amsterdam. She was broken up in Hamburg during 1970.

Fairfield Shipbuilding and Engineering Co. Ltd., Govan; 1948, 11,252gt, 506 feet
Two four-cylinder 2SCSA oil engines by Fairfield Shipbuilding and Engineering Co. Ltd., Govan driving twin screws

AUREOL

In post-war years, Elder, Dempster built three diesel-driven passenger ships for its service from Liverpool to West Africa, the sisters *Apapa* and *Accra,* and the somewhat larger *Aureol,* seen here mid-river on a sunny day. Although diesel engines were quite innovative for passengers ships, even immediately after the war, in some respects the three ships were anachronistic. For instance, despite voyaging to the tropics, they were not fitted with air conditioning throughout their accommodation until 1960.

In March 1972 *Aureol* had the dubious distinction of being the last ocean-going passenger ship to sail from Liverpool on a liner service. She then shifted her terminal to Southampton.

Sold by Elder, Dempster in 1974, she became an accommodation ship in the Middle East under the name *Marianna VI.* This lasted until 1991, when she was laid up in Greek waters from where she was sent to breakers in India during 2001. She had spent more than half of her 50-year life in a static role, either as an accommodation ship or in lay up.

Alexander Stephen and Sons Ltd., Glasgow; 1951, 14,083gt, 537 feet
Two four-cylinder 2SCSA oil engines by Alexander Stephen and Sons Ltd., Glasgow driving twin screws

APAPA

Seen ready to go alongside the Princes Landing Stage to load passengers, Elder, Dempster's *Apapa* made 177 voyages before succumbing to competition from air travel in 1968. She was then sold to a Hong Kong owner who presumably used her along the coast of China, renaming her *Taipooshan*. She ended her days with Taiwan shipbreakers in 1975. Her sister *Accra* was not to find a second career, and was broken up in Spain in 1967.

Vickers Armstrongs Ltd., Barrow-in-Furness; 1948, 11,607gt, 471 feet
Two Doxford-type four-cylinder 4SCSA oil engines by Vickers Armstrongs Ltd., Barrow-in-Furness driving twin screws

ONITSHA

Faced with increasing competition from specialist heavy-lift ships (see *Christen Smith* on page 57), British cargo liner companies such as Elder, Dempster increasingly tried to accommodate traffic such as railway locomotives. *Onitsha* was the lead ship of three specially designed for such heavy cargoes: note the massive size of her two heavy-lift derricks. The other members of the trio were *Obuasi* (the company's cadet ship for some years) and *Owerri*.

Onitsha was sold in 1972 to Greek owners to become *Amvourgon*. In January 1975 she had a fire in the engine room whilst coasting down from Quebec to Baltimore, and her crew abandoned ship. The 20-year-old ship was taken in tow and brought into Halifax. Declared a complete loss, she was towed across the Atlantic to Santander in Spain for demolition.

Harland and Wolff Ltd., Belfast; 1952, 5,802gt, 449 feet
Five-cylinder 2SCSA Burmeister & Wain-type oil engine by Harland and Wolff Ltd., Belfast

WARWICKSHIRE

Bibby Line are one of Liverpool's - and, indeed, the world's - oldest shipowners, John Bibby buying his first ship in 1801, exactly 200 years ago. For much of this time, the Bibby ships ran a cargo and passenger service from Liverpool and Birkenhead to Rangoon and Colombo, and became known for their magnificently elegant four-masted passenger steamers and motor ships.

Warwickshire changed all this. From four masts, she came down to just one, and in place of diesels she had a steam turbine. Trade was changing too, and with the post-war independence of Burma and its increasing estrangement from Britain, *Warwickshire's* capacity for 76 passengers became increasingly irrelevant. When the passenger service ended in 1965 she was sold, and underwent a heroic conversion to a car ferry. As *Hania* she worked between Piraeus and Crete until her sister *Leicestershire* - also converted to a car ferry as *Heraklion* - capsized with the loss of over 200 lives in December 1966. Their owners, Typaldos Brothers, were forced into bankruptcy, and *Hania* rotted away in a Greek anchorage until sold for scrap.

Fairfield Shipbuilding and Engineering Co. Ltd., Govan; 1948, 8,903gt, 498 feet

Two steam turbines by Fairfield Shipbuilding and Engineering Co. Ltd., Govan driving twin screws

HEREFORDSHIRE

One of Bibby's first pure cargo ships for many years, *Herefordshire* was designed in such a way that she could be converted into a passenger ship if trade warranted it. Alas, it did not, and even cargo carrying on Bibby's Burma route could not offer her full employment. As a result, she was chartered to Port Line for seven years as *Port Hardy*.

But towards the end of her career the idea of converting her for passenger carrying resurfaced. Greek owners bought her in 1969 and renamed her *Merryland*. Transferred to the Cyprus flag, she was to become a cruise ship, but the idea was abandoned and she was broken up in Taiwan during 1973.

In the background of this photograph can just be seen a Bibby ship of an older generation, the four-masted *Oxfordshire* of 1912.

Barclay, Curle and Co. Ltd., Whiteinch, Glasgow; 1944, 8,311gt, 493 feet
Two four-cylinder 2SCSA oil engines by Barclay, Curle and Co. Ltd., Whiteinch, Glasgow driving twin screws

EMPIRE PRIDE

Empire Pride had a distinguished wartime career as a troopship, and went on to give excellent service in peacetime. She could carry 2,200 troops, a capacity which was used in landings in Madagascar, North Africa, Sicily and the South of France. After hostilities ended she continued trooping until 1954, but now carried just 1,600 - some relief, but still a tight fit. She was managed by Bibby Line, whose long and distinguished record of running troopships continued into the 1960s.

On her sale by the Ministry of Transport in June 1954, *Empire Pride* was sent to Lubeck to be converted to a cargo ship, becoming *Charlton Pride* for the Chandris Group. Within 18 months she had been bought by Donaldson Line, who had her further refitted to carry just 12 passengers plus 800 head of lifestock. As *Calgaria* she ran between the UK and Canada until 1963 when sold to Greek owners who renamed her *Embassy*, loaded her with scrap in Liverpool and sent her to Hong Kong breakers.

Barclay, Curle and Co. Ltd., Whiteinch, Glasgow; 1941, 9,248gt, 495 feet
Two four-cylinder 2SCSA oil engines by Barclay, Curle and Co. Ltd., Whiteinch, Glasgow driving twin screws

ASTYANAX

Blue Funnel were almost synonymous with Mersey shipping in the 1950s, and usually had at least four or five of their magnificent cargo ships in Birkenhead and in Gladstone Dock. Founder Alfred Holt had pioneered the use of steamships on the long haul to the Far East. Adopting innovations such as compound engines and higher boiler pressures, he ensured that his ships were economical enough to compete with sailing ships. The company he founded - officially the Ocean Steam Ship Co. Ltd., but usually known as Blue Funnel - went on to be what many felt was the world's greatest cargo liner company, with standards so high that they did not need to insure their ships against marine risks.

The A class, of which *Astyanax* is an example, became the backbone of the fleet in 1950s and 1960s, a class of 21 motor ships developed from a pre-war design which met the company's needs almost to the end of their conventional liner services. Integral to their design, and to their appeal to onlookers, was a magnificent blue funnel.

Astyanax spent five years with Glen Line from 1957 to 1962 as *Glenfruin*, but reverted to *Astyanax* until broken up at Kaohsiung in December 1972.

Scotts' Shipbuilding and Engineering Co. Ltd., Greenock; 1948, 7,648gt, 463 feet

Eight-cylinder 2SCDA oil engine by J.G. Kincaid and Co. Ltd., Greenock

DEUCALION

This rather elderly motor ship looks nothing like a traditional Blue Funnel vessel. The *Deucalion* came into the fleet as a result of Holts buying one of its major competitors, Glen Line Ltd., in 1935. Glen Line's attraction was its strong position in the Far East trade from ports on the East Coast of the UK, including London, whereas Blue Funnel was a predominantly West Coast company. For Glen Line crews, the takeover meant improved conditions to match those of Blue Funnel personnel. It was, in fact, a merger in all but name, as the Glen Line title had some goodwill and - more importantly - rights in the freight conferences that determined how many ships could run in a given trade.

In February 1949 transfers between the companies began, and saw *Glenogle* become Blue Funnel's *Deucalion*. As new tonnage arrived, she was sold for scrap and broken up at Briton Ferry in 1956.

Harland and Wolff Ltd; Glasgow, 1920, 9,513gt, 486 feet.
Two eight-cylinder 4SCSA oil engines by Harland and Wolff Ltd; Glasgow driving twin screws

PATROCLUS

Blue Funnel wanted to be able to claim they had the fastest ships on the Far East service, but in the early 1950s a single marine diesel could not give the desired service speed of 18 knots. Rather than suffer the expense and complexity of two engines and twin screws, they reverted to steam turbines for their four P class passenger-cargo ships. They loaded at Birkenhead, collected more cargo from Rotterdam, and then sailed non-stop to Singapore in the very brisk time of 20 days. With a round trip taking four months, the quartet could offer a monthly service to the Far East.

These 10,000-ton cargo ships, with their accommodation for 35 passengers, did much to re-establish Blue Funnel's supremacy after the war. Possibly for some sentimental reason, *Patroclus* was renamed *Philoctetes* in 1972 for her final voyage to shipbreakers at Kaohsiung.

Vickers-Armstrongs Ltd., Newcastle-upon-Tyne; 1950, 10,109gt, 516 feet
Three steam turbines by Vickers-Armstrongs Ltd., Newcastle-upon-Tyne driving a single screw

TRADER

T. and J. Harrison were one of the liner companies that made Liverpool shipping great. Never owning any big or prestigious passenger ships, they nevertheless established a reputation for solid reliability, thanks to prudent investment in ships of the right size for their trades and, of course, the dedication of their predominantly Liverpool-based officers and crews.

Harrisons' fleet in the 1950s was rather traditional looking, and *Trader* has the very tall funnel typical of a ship with natural draught, and which relied on a high smoke stack to keep the furnaces drawing, rather than the use of fans. By the end of the decade steamships like *Trader* were obsolescent, and in 1961 she was sold to flag-of-convenience owners and as *Pemto* made just one voyage to Hong Kong and the breakers.

Charles Connell and Co. Ltd., Glasgow; 1940, 6,143gt, 435 feet
T. 3-cyl. by David Rowan and Co. Ltd., Glasgow

BIOGRAPHER

Harrison's steamers first operated a service to the brandy-producing regions of France. This was reflected in the name adopted for the company which owned their ships - the Charente Steamship Co. Ltd. In post-war years, and with the brandy trade ended, the company's name was something of an anomaly as the ships now served India, South Africa and the Caribbean.

Over the years, Harrisons used a wonderful variety of names which can best be described as reflecting 'positions' in life, or perhaps 'callings'. These ran from *Student* to *Patrician*, and from *Workman* to *Statesman*. The name *Biographer* was used just once, for one of the first class of ships built after the Second World War.

Sold in 1964 she ran under the Lebanese flag as *Tolmi* until 1973 when machinery damage led to her being broken up.

Lithgows Ltd., Port Glasgow; 1949, 6,922gt, 464 feet
Two steam turbines by David Rowan and Co. Ltd., Glasgow driving a single screw

JOURNALIST

By the mid-1950s, Harrison Line ships had developed a distinctly new appearance, with sloping tops to their funnels, composite superstructure, a long forecastle and usually a heavy-lift derrick on the foremast. *Journalist,* like most of Harrison's post-war ships, was built and engined by Doxfords of Sunderland.

When sold in 1973 she went to the inevitable Greek owner as *Aghia Thalassini*. She became *Elissar* in 1981 for one last voyage to Gadani Beach near Karachi, where in the 1980s so many ships were broken up under horrendous working conditions.

William Doxford and Sons Ltd., Sunderland; 1954, 8,366gt, 465 feet
Four-cylinder 2SCSA oil engine by William Doxford and Sons Ltd., Sunderland

MAIPURA

T. and J. Brocklebank Ltd., another of Liverpool's long-established shipowners, were very proud of their tradition of flying their houseflag from the foremast (where it can just be seen in this photograph), rather than the mainmast where most other owners flew it. A white-painted strake seen on *Maipura's* hull was another distinctive feature of a Brocklebank ship.

       Since 1919, the company had been controlled by Cunard Line who wanted a stake in services to India, Brocklebanks having become the major company in the trade from the UK to Calcutta.

       Maipura was the first ship built for Brocklebanks with a composite rather than a split superstructure, intended to make it easier to

stow bulkier items of deck cargo such as the locomotives and rolling stock. This design was later developed by adopting bipod masts whose two stout legs made lifting such heavy items easier.

       Maipura was distinguished by a particularly tall funnel - the original had been lengthened by 12 feet after completion to try to prevent fumes from the engine room entering her accommodation.

       Maipura was sold in 1972 and after two years sailing under the Panama flag as *Liberty Retailer* was broken up in Taiwan.

William Hamilton and Co. Ltd., Port Glasgow; 1952, 9,748gt, 509 feet
Three steam turbines by David Rowan and Co. Ltd., Glasgow driving a single screw

NOVA SCOTIA

Although no bigger than the average cargo ship, *Nova Scotia* was in fact a fully-fledged North Atlantic liner. She and her sister *Newfoundland* had accommodation for around 155 passengers as well as cargo space and were for the Johnston Warren Line service from Liverpool to St. Johns, Newfoundland, Halifax and Boston. Around 80 crew serviced these passengers: a relatively modest number when it is recalled that in the early 1950s a Shell tanker required almost as many with not a passenger in sight.

The North Atlantic could be an uncomfortable place in such a modest ship, so it is hardly surprising that airliners soon took this passenger trade. In 1961 *Nova Scotia's* owners, who were part of the Furness Group as can be seen from the funnel markings, bowed to the inevitable and reduced the passenger numbers to 12, the number often found on cargo liners because it meant that a doctor did not have to be carried. But Johnston Warren also took the step of building for the service two new, cargo-only motor vessels, which inherited the names *Nova Scotia* and *Newfoundland*.

The original *Nova Scotia* and *Newfoundland* found new roles on the opposite side of the world. After refits on the Clyde in 1962 they went to an Australian owner for a monthly cargo-passenger service from Australia via Hong Kong and China to Japan. Renamed *Francis Drake* and *George Anson*, they remained on this service until broken up within weeks of each other at Taiwan in 1971.

Vickers-Armstrongs Ltd., Newcastle-upon-Tyne; 1947, 7,438gt, 441 feet
Three steam turbines by Vickers-Armstrongs Ltd., Barrow-in-Furness driving a single screw

19

CYPRIAN PRINCE

Cyprian Prince belonged to the Prince Line which was the brainchild of James Knott, one of Britain's most remarkable shipping entrepreneurs. A grocer's son from Newcastle, Knott came relatively late to shipping. He built his first steamer in 1881, but within a decade was operating on routes to the Mediterranean and had services to North and South America which developed into a round-the-world service. Knott was also a pioneer of the oil tanker. He sold out to the Furness Group in 1916, shattered by the loss of his sons during the war, but ships with *Prince* names and the Prince of Wales feathers on their funnels remained a familiar sight on Merseyside until the 1970s.

Cyprian Prince ran for 18 years, mainly to the Mediterranean, until she was sold. As one Greek owner passed her to another, she took the names *Agios Dionisios*, then *Irene's Wish*, and lastly *Fulmartrader*. In January 1976 she was abandoned by her crew in the Mediterranean when a fire broke out in her engine room. She was first towed into Palma, from where she was taken in tow for Piraeus where it was intended to repair her. However, her ageing hulk sank off Palermo on 14th February.
Burntisland Shipbuilding Co. Ltd., Burntisland; 1949, 2,358gt, 334 feet Three-cylinder 2SCSA oil engine by Hawthorn, Leslie and Co. Ltd., Newcastle-upon-Tyne

NORTHUMBRIAN PRINCE

The small but beautifully formed cargo liner *Northumbrian Prince* would have been on the Manchester to the Mediterranean service jointly operated by Prince Line and Manchester Liners. Sold after just 12 years' service, the little motor vessel readily found further employment, and under the names *Eleftherotria, Rodania, Omar, Suraj* and finally *Karari* survived until 1985 when she was broken up on Gadani Beach near Karachi.

Burntisland Shipbuilding Co. Ltd., Burntisland; 1956, 2,709gt, 335 feet
Four-cylinder 2SCSA Doxford oil engine by Ailsa Shipbuilding Co. Ltd., Troon

MANCHESTER PROGRESS

When the Manchester Ship Canal was fully opened in 1895, it was hailed as a masterpiece of engineering and a credit to the determination of Manchester. But a great commercial success it was not. Shipowners were wary of sending their ships all the way to Manchester, when they could save several days by using Liverpool. Manchester's response was to go into partnership with Christopher Furness, one of the leading shipping entrepreneurs of his day, to form Manchester Liners Ltd. The company ran services to Canada and the Great Lakes, and also to the Mediterranean.

Manchester Progress was one of a group of turbine ships with which Manchester Liners re-equipped itself in the late 1930s as the depression was ending. She survived Atlantic convoys - no mean achievement - and soldiered on until replaced in 1966 by the first generation of container ships, which the company pioneered. *Manchester Progress* was broken up in Yugoslavia.

Blythswood Shipbuilding Co. Ltd., Glasgow; 1938, 7,281gt, 447 feet
Three steam turbines by David Rowan and Co. Ltd., Glasgow driving a single screw

SCOTTISH STAR

The funnels of Blue Star ships like *Scottish Star* were built particularly big to show off the company's splendid colours. This is surprising as the Vestey Group, who owned Blue Star, were rather secretive about their affairs. Vesteys were originally meat traders and cold store owners but came to control at least three major shipping lines.

Scottish Star was one of the 15 unfortunate ships to be trapped in the Great Bitter Lakes when the Suez Canal was blocked during the Arab-Israeli conflict of June 1967. The war lasted just six days, in stark contrast to her detention which lasted eight years: she was not released until May 1975. Greek owners then bought her from the insurers to whom she had been abandoned, but although she was renamed *Kavo Yerakas* she never traded again. She was laid up until 1979 when broken up in Spain, having been idle for 12 of her 29 years.

Fairfield Shipbuilding and Engineering Co. Ltd., Govan; 1950, 9,996gt, 505 feet
Two five-cylinder 2SCSA oil engines by Fairfield Shipbuilding and Engineering Co. Ltd., Govan driving a single screw

SPENSER

Spenser's owners, Lamport and Holt, were another Liverpool institution. The company was almost as important in the South American trade as Blue Funnel was to the Far East. By the 1950s, however, they had lost a lot of their prestige, partly through being part of the Royal Mail Group which crashed so disastrously in the years between the wars, and partly because since 1944 they had been effectively a subsidiary of Blue Star Line.

Bought by Lamport and Holt in 1950, *Spenser* had lived through interesting times. She was built for the South American service of Norddeutscher Lloyd, and was captured by the Royal Navy off Valparaiso in December 1939. As *Poland* and later *Empire Confidence* she ran for the Government throughout the war, and was then chartered to Egypt as *Star of El Nil*. After just five years with Lamport and Holt *Spenser's* name was needed for a new ship, and as *Roscoe* she sailed on until broken up in Spain during 1962.

Bremer Vulkan, Vegesack, Germany; 1935, 6,334gt, 430 feet
Six-cylinder 2SCDA oil engine by Bremer Vulkan, Vegesack, Germany

VIANNA

Not all Basil Feilden's photographs were taken on perfect days, but as *Vianna* is manoeuvred by her tugs into Liverpool docks, the sun breaks through to illuminate a choppy Mersey.

Vianna was a little ship which made big voyages: from Liverpool to ports in the Amazon basin on charter to the Booth Line. As well as big passenger ships (see *Hildebrand* below), Booth used ships of *Vianna's* size to serve smaller ports on the Amazon. Her design, with clear spaces between her masts that had been intended to simplify the carrying of military equipment (see page 46), would have suited her to lift deck cargoes of large logs.

She had been completed as *Rockwood Park*, and her first commercial owners renamed her, somewhat exuberantly, *La Grande Hermine*. As *Vianna* she was owned by the Panama Shipping Co., a subsidiary of the Vestey Group who also owned Booth Line, from 1951 to 1955, when she went to owners in Oran, Algeria as *Cap Falcon*. She ended her days under the Italian flag as *Licola*, being broken up at La Spezia in 1971.

St. John Dry Dock and Shipbuilding Co. Ltd., St. John, New Brunswick; 1943, 2,825gt, 328 feet
T. 3-cyl. by the Dominion Bridge Co. Ltd., Montreal

HILDEBRAND

Hildebrand was one of those fine ships which came to a premature end. Along with her sister *Hubert* of 1955, she operated for Booth Line on a passenger-cargo service from Liverpool which took her first to Lisbon, then across the Atlantic to Para in Brazil and then up the Amazon as far as Manaos. In September 1957, the less than six years old *Hildebrand* was entering Lisbon in thick fog when she ran onto rocks. Fortunately the crew and all 164 passengers were rescued, but despite attempts to pull her off, *Hildebrand* became a total loss. Her passengers had to be picked up from Lisbon by the much older Booth Liner *Hilary*.

Hildebrand's younger sister *Hubert*, which also had the large Thorneycroft-design funnel, continued on the service until 1964, by when airliners were making serious inroads into passenger carrying.

Cammell, Laird and Co. Ltd., Birkenhead; 1951, 7,735gt, 439 feet
Two steam turbines by Cammell, Laird and Co. Ltd., Birkenhead driving a single screw

CLAN CHATTAN

Serving South Africa and India, Clan liners were almost as familiar as Blue Funnellers on the Birkenhead side of the river, where the two companies shared Vittoria Dock. Although owned in Glasgow, Clan liners such as *Clan Chattan* were a welcome sight on Merseyside. They were generally in immaculate condition, and were instantly recognisable with their generous areas of white paint, a sober but attractive black funnel with two red bands, and unusual grey masts.

The Cayzer family, who made their fortune through Clan Line, were another of Britain's shipping dynasties, and came to buy such famous companies as Union-Castle and King Line, as well as having their own shipyard at Greenock.

Clan Chattan was a no-frills wartime version of a design from the 1930s, the *Clan Cameron*-class built to the maximum dimensions for the docks at Calcutta. *She* was sold for scrap in 1962, reaching Hong Kong and the breakers on 14th May 1962.

Greenock Dockyard Co. Ltd., Greenock; 1944, 9,585gt, 488 feet
Two T. 3-cyl. with low-pressure turbines by J.G. Kincaid and Co. Ltd., Greenock driving twin screws

HALIZONES

The Houston Line had a long-established service to South America and was taken over by Clan Line at the end of the First World War when Houston was demoralised by war losses, and Clan Line desperate for tonnage for the same reason. The acquisition gave Clan, which mostly served India, a useful new route.

The *Halizones* was a superannuated Clan liner transferred to Houston ownership, having been the *Clan Murray* for almost thirty years when transferred in 1948. Not surprisingly, she gave only four years' service before being broken up on the Firth of Forth.

Ayrshire Dockyard Co. Ltd., Irvine; 1919, 5,954gt, 425 feet
T. 3-cyl. with low-pressure turbine by Dunsmuir and Jackson Ltd., Glasgow

HESPERIDES

Moving in the opposite direction to *Halizones*, the *Hesperides* began service as a Houston ship, and was transferred to Clan Line towards the end of her days. Also in contrast to *Halizones*, she wears Clan Line's funnel.

Hesperides was actually a wartime standard ship of the C type, readily recognisable by her composite superstructure, with no hatch between the engine room and bridge. She was launched for the Ministry of War Transport as *Empire Longstone*, but was completed as *Hesperides* for Houston Line.

When transferred to Clan Line in 1960, she took the name *Clan Murray*. This name had not been used since the third *Clan Murray* became *Halizones* in 1948. She went to breakers in Japan in 1962.

Shipbuilding Corporation Ltd. (Wear Branch), Sunderland; 1946, 7,301gt, 449 feet
T. 3-cyl by George Clark (1938) Ltd., Sunderland

CITY OF LONDON

The Ellerman Group was made up of six separate shipping companies in various trades, all acquired by financier John Ellerman. Five of the companies had a similar colour scheme: white and grey hulls with white topside strakes and red below the waterline, with a yellow, white and black funnel. Distinctive houseflags allowed the ships of the five individual companies to be told apart. The sixth company, Ellerman's Wilson Line, kept its original colour scheme.

City of London, one of a class of five split between the companies, went to Ellerman and Bucknall for their South African services. She was chosen to represent Ellerman during the Coronation Review at Spithead in June 1953.

City of London was sold early in 1967, and ran for Greek owners as *Sandra N* until arriving at the breakers in Taiwan at the end of 1968.
Swan, Hunter and Wigham Richardson Ltd., Wallsend-on-Tyne; 1947, 8,434gt, 500 feet
Six sets of steam turbines by Wallsend Slipway Co. Ltd., Wallsend-on-Tyne driving twin screws

CITY OF OTTAWA

City of Ottawa was the last of a large class of turbine steamers delivered to the Hall and City Lines from 1948, and which very much shaped the appearance of the Ellerman fleet which used Birkenhead's West Float.

　　City of Ottawa was renamed *City of Leeds* in 1971 to release the name for a newer ship which was to serve Canadian routes. Sold in 1975, she became *Gulf Venture* for owners who originated in Pakistan. However,

the complexities of turbine steamers and their thirst for fuel did not endear them to third-world owners, and *Gulf Venture* was broken up on Gadani Beach, Pakistan in 1977.

Vickers-Armstrongs Ltd., Newcastle-upon-Tyne; 1950, 7,622gt, 485 feet
Three steam turbines by Vickers-Armstrongs Ltd., Newcastle-upon-Tyne
driving a single screw

CORINTHIAN

Wartime losses of ships and men by companies like Ellerman and Papayanni Lines were nothing short of horrendous. For instance, out of a class of six steamers built for their Mediterranean routes just before the war, four were lost through torpedoes, bombs, and mines. *Corinthian* - seen here - and *Pandorian* were the two survivors. The former saw out her days with the company, and was still wearing its colours when sold to Scottish shipbreakers in 1963.

The design of these modest-sized but handsome steamers was developed in post-war years, with six ships of the *Egyptian* class. Externally, they lost the wooden-fronted bridge, and internally they differed in having steam turbine machinery. *William Gray and Co. Ltd., West Hartlepool; 1938, 3,198gt, 359 feet*
T. 3-cyl with low-pressure turbine by Central Marine Engine Works, West Hartlepool

LUCIAN

Soon after the war, Ellerman and Papayanni Lines had a class of five small twin-screw motorships built for their service from the United Kingdom to Portugal. The high degree of autonomy given to individual Ellerman companies is evident from the fact that the Group was simultaneously taking delivery of vessels powered by diesel engines, by steam reciprocating engines, and by turbines.

The five motorships were named *Crosbian, Darinian, Lucian* (seen here), *Mercian* and *Palmelian*. All had respectable careers, and after *Lucian* was sold in 1964 she completed another 16 years' service as *Amorgos, Yashoo* and *Gulf Star* before being broken up.
William Gray and Co. Ltd., West Hartlepool; 1948, 1,516gt, 272 feet
Two six-cylinder 2SCSA oil engines by British Polar Diesels Ltd., Glasgow driving twin screws

CUZCO

Liverpool shipping companies could take credit for opening up major regions of the world to trade. The Pacific Steam Navigation Company, for instance, was largely responsible for bringing steamships to the west coast of South America. Ironically, the founder was a United States citizen, William Wheelwright, who turned to Britain when he failed to find financial support at home. The company moved to Liverpool from London in the 1840s, and their ships became so familiar in the docks on the Wirral side of the river that the company became known as 'the Birkenhead Navy'.

However, *Cuzco* and her post-war running mates would have been more familiar in the docks on the Liverpool side. *Cuzco* was not ordered by Pacific Steam, but purchased on the stocks from another Liverpool owner, James Chambers and Co. who intended to name her *Thurland Castle*. When Pacific Steam sold *Cuzco* in 1965, the ship began a second career sailing to the Far East for Ben Line of Glasgow as *Benattow*, as which she continued to visit the Mersey until 1977 when broken up in Taiwan.

Blyth Dry Docks and Shipbuilding Co. Ltd., Blyth; 1951, 8,038gt, 501 feet Three steam turbines by Parson's Marine Steam Turbine Co. Ltd., Wallsend-on-Tyne driving a single screw

CAPTAIN HOBSON

Few ships can have carried such a variety of passenger as *Captain Hobson*. First there were the colonials: she was built soon after the First World War as *Amarapoora* for Henderson Line to carry officials and their families to and from their postings in Burma.

In 1939 *Amarapoora* became a hospital ship, initially based at Scapa Flow, but active during the evacuation of Norway. She was later present at the North African landings, at Salerno and finally - after having air conditioning fitted - worked in the Far East.

Her next group of passengers were prisoners of war who were being repatriated. She then ran between Italy and Australia with displaced persons and refugees, also doing some trooping.

In 1951 her owners - the Ministry of Transport - sent her to the Clyde to be refitted to carry migrants on assisted passage schemes to New Zealand. For this she became *Captain Hobson* and, managed by former owners Henderson Line, made 12 voyages before her retirement in 1958. As no buyers could be found, she was broken up in Japan in 1959.

William Denny and Brothers Ltd., Dumbarton; 1920, 9,306gt, 485 feet
T. 3-cyl. by William Denny and Brothers Ltd., Dumbarton

YOMA

If a country possessed a port, the chances were that a Liverpool ship could be found which traded to it. For instance, Burma had services from two companies which used the Mersey, 'Paddy' Henderson of Glasgow and Liverpool's own Bibby Line.

Henderson's *Yoma* was a slightly old-fashioned-looking cargo ship, with a hold between the engine room and bridge that could never have been easy to work. She is recorded as having a crew of 78, a remarkable number by today's standards, when a ship of several times her size would have a dozen at most.

Hendersons were taken over by Elder, Dempster of Liverpool in 1952. However, *Yoma* continued on the same service from Glasgow and Birkenhead to Rangoon until Nationalist Chinese owners bought her in 1964. As *Hai Ping* she then ran on a liner service from Taiwan to New York until broken up in 1970.

William Denny and Brothers Ltd., Dumbarton; 1948, 5,809gt, 463 feet

Three steam turbines by William Denny and Brothers Ltd., Dumbarton driving a single screw

SALWEEN

Henderson's *Salween* and her sister *Prome* were passenger and cargo carriers, and so offered their hundred or so passengers a more relaxed atmosphere on their voyage to Asia than the big P.&O. liners. But when *Salween* worked as a troopship during the war, her 1,400 service men were carried in much less comfort. She made a voyage out to Port Said via the Cape, helped to evacuate Commonwealth troops from Greece, and then worked in East African waters during the successful campaign against the Italians.

Returning to the Burmese trade after the war, she and *Prome* stuck it out until 1962, when their erstwhile passengers began to desert ships for airliners. She then made a last voyage out to Hong Kong where she was broken up.

William Denny and Brothers Ltd., Dumbarton; 1938, 7,063gt, 462 feet

Three steam turbines by William Denny and Brothers Ltd., Dumbarton driving a single screw

DORELIAN

Dorelian is a reminder of long-gone Liverpool shipowners, Frederick Leyland and Co. Ltd. This company owned Bibby Line for many years, eventually selling it back to the family. When Leyland Line was split up in 1934 its ships went to T. and J. Harrison, and its goodwill and name to the Vestey Group. Ellerman had already taken up Leyland's naming scheme for its smaller ships running to the Mediterranean.

Harrisons sold *Dorelian* to Donaldson Line in 1936, and she survived until 1954 when she was taken to Dalmuir for scrapping, still carrying the name she had been built with over thirty years earlier.
D. and W. Henderson and Co. Ltd., Glasgow; 1923, 6,431gt, 400 feet
Q. 4-cyl. by D. and W. Henderson and Co. Ltd., Glasgow

LISMORIA

Donaldson Line was a medium-sized Glasgow-based company that operated services to South America and to Canada. Like many others, they lacked the resources to make the massive investment needed for containerisation, and decided to get out of shipping, selling their remaining fleet in 1967.

Lismoria, one of the last to go, was an unusual ship. Completed as the troopship *Taos Victory,* in 1946 she was transferred without change of name to the British Ministry of Transport. Donaldson bought her in 1948 and modified her to accommodate 55 passengers. With her sister *Laurentia* she maintained sailings from Glasgow to Montreal, but during the months when the St. Lawrence River was iced over, the two ships made a round trip from Glasgow and Liverpool to Los Angeles, San Francisco, Victoria and Vancouver. The low winter sunlight in this photograph suggests that *Lismoria's* visit to the Mersey was during one of these voyages.

Lismoria was sold in January 1967, a Greek owner renaming her *Neon* for a final voyage, probably laden with scrap, to Taiwan and the shipbreakers.

California Shipbuilding Corporation, Los Angeles, USA; 1945, 8,323gt, 455 feet
Two steam turbines by the General Electric Company, Lynn, Massachusetts, USA driving a single screw

BENCLEUCH

Ben Line Steamers Ltd. were an Edinburgh company which served the Far East, and as such were always a thorn in the side of the much larger Blue Funnel Line. Ben Line specialised in fast ships: *Bencleuch* was one of their first post-war class, which could easily manage 16 knots. Later ships were faster still.

Bencleuch had a long and, one hopes, profitable career, being broken up not far from Ben Line's base on the Firth of Forth in 1972.

Charles Connell and Co. Ltd., Glasgow; 1949, 7,868gt, 475 feet
Two steam turbines by David Rowan and Co. Ltd., Glasgow driving a single screw

ARMANISTAN

Strick Line was one of the principal companies serving ports in the Persian Gulf. It is amusing to remember - given the amount of oil now produced by this region - that the earliest sailings by Strick Line carried coal out to the Gulf. The developing oil industry certainly helped the company, which expanded in the 1950s to carry equipment for the oilfields.

Armanistan is on one of Strick's regular sailings from Manchester, and displays to perfection Strick's striking and colourful funnel, with alternating red and blue chevrons.

Increasing nationalism in shipping, with Persian Gulf countries in particular building up their own shipping fleets, caused problems for Strick in the 1960s, and *Armanistan* with her outdated steam engines was sold in 1965. Her subsequent names were *Mitera Maria* and *Marbella*, but a fire in the engine room hastened her end and she was broken up on Gadani Beach near Karachi in 1974.
John Readhead and Sons Ltd., South Shields; 1949, 8,409gt, 512 feet
T. 3-cyl. with low pressure turbine by John Readhead and Sons Ltd., South Shields

TAKORADI PALM

One look at the funnel of this ship gives away the name of its owner: Palm Line Ltd. The company originated as the United Africa Co. Ltd. when soap manufacturers Lever Brothers decided to have their own ships to bring raw materials - principally palm oil - from West Africa to their works at Bromborough.

Unusually, she was built in Germany because her owners had considerable funds in that country which the Nazi government would not let them take out, and the solution was to have ships built in German yards. As *Takoradian* she survived the war, although she was detained at Dakar by the Vichy French and operated by them as *St. Paul* until released in 1943, after which the British Government ran her for a while as *Empire Swale*. In 1949 she was given her new name *Takoradi Palm* after the setting up of Palm Line Ltd. She served the company until 1959 when the almost inevitable Greek owner bought her and ran her for four more years as *Irini's Luck*. She was broken up in 1963.
Deutsche Schiff-und Masch. A.G. Seebeck, Wesermunde, Germany; 1937, 5,452gt, 439 feet
Two six-cylinder 2SCSA oil engines by Deutsche Schiff-und Masch. A.G. Weser, Wesermunde, Germany driving a single screw

TAMAROA

Shaw, Savill and Albion Line was the oldest company serving New Zealand, and many of those who served on their ships felt that they were run on very traditional lines. Conditions for officers and crew were not always of the best, and they claimed that the initials SSA stood for 'slow starvation and agony'.

During part of its long life, the company had been owned by the famous White Star Line, and inherited several ships from another old-established antipodean trader, the Aberdeen Line, which was also partly owned by White Star. One such was *Sophocles*, which was given the traditional Shaw, Savill name *Tamaroa* in 1926.

Tamaroa had an exciting war. As a troopship, she was the commodore's vessel in a convoy which was attacked on Christmas Day 1940 by the German heavy cruiser *Admiral Hipper*. Fortunately, however, the cruiser made off when *HMS Berwick* appeared. *Tamaroa* went on to serve in the North African landings.

By August 1948 she was back on Shaw, Savill's routes, carrying up to 372 tourist-class passengers. The old lady completed her final voyage in October 1956, and the next year was sent to Blyth to be broken up.

Harland and Wolff Ltd., Belfast; 1922, 12,375gt, 500 feet
Four Brown-Curtis-Harland and Wolff steam turbines by Harland and Wolff Ltd., Belfast driving twin screws

GOTHIC

Immediately after the war, Shaw, Savill ordered a class of four cargo-passenger ships which took names inherited from its one-time parent, White Star: the *Athenic, Corinthic, Ceramic,* and *Gothic.* The last of these was selected for use as the yacht for a royal tour planned to begin in 1952, and was sent back to her builders to be titivated for the task. With the death of King George VI, the tour was postponed, but *Gothic* was left in white royal yacht livery, as seen here. The royal tour got underway late in 1953, with *Gothic* manned by a normal Shaw, Savill crew, even carrying cargo between some of the ports. Nevertheless, the cost of this junket was a cool £850,000.

Gothic returned to her normal service, her passenger traffic no doubt benefiting from her royal patronage. Like many cargo-passenger ships, however, her career was not long, and she was broken up in 1969.

Swan, Hunter and Wigham Richardsson Ltd., Wallsend-on-Tyne; 1948, 15,902gt, 561 feet
Six steam turbines by Wallsend Slipway Co. Ltd., Newcastle-upon-Tyne driving twin screws

RANGITIKI

The New Zealand Shipping Co. Ltd. was formed way back in 1873 by New Zealand farmers who wanted some control over the rates charged to ship their produce to the UK. Initially they ran only sailing ships, and could only build steamers if they received a subsidy from the New Zealand Government. When subsidies were withdrawn due to a trade depression, the company was only rescued from financial disaster when a British businessman stepped in, and from 1890 the company was run from London.

In the 1920s the New Zealand company built three passenger ships which were considered a bold step in that they were fitted with diesel engines. In fact, they proved an excellent investment, and the two which survived the war, *Rangitiki* and her sister *Rangitata*, traded until 1962 when they were broken up. However, *Rangitiki's* career almost ended in November 1940 when her convoy was attacked by the German pocket-battleship *Admiral Scheer*. She was only saved by the self sacrifice of the escorting *Jervis Bay* which, although completely outgunned, fought the big German warship until she sank. Her action allowed most of the ships to scatter in the darkness of a November night.

John Brown and Co. Ltd., Clydebank; 1929, 16,984gt, 552 feet
Two six-cylinder 2SCSA oil engines by John Brown and Co. Ltd., Clydebank driving twin screws

RAKAIA

Harland and Wolff's Belfast yard built a number of refrigerator ships towards the end of the Second World War, all of which found ready buyers amongst British liner companies whose war losses had been nothing less than horrific. *Empire Abercorn* was bought by the New Zealand Shipping Co. Ltd. in 1946 and became *Rakaia*. She had been fitted with fairly basic accommodation for 45 passengers, and her new owners turned this into cabins for 40 cadets.

During October 1957, *Rakaia* was a day and a half out of New York when a piston rod broke, disabling her engine and leaving her capable of only three knots. To steady the ship, and perhaps give her an extra half knot, the cadets were set to make sails from hatchcovers. Those on board remember shortages of food and fresh water, and that only the engine room staff - working hard to keep her going - were allowed showers and bacon and eggs!

Rakaia was broken up in Hong Kong during 1971.

Harland and Wolff Ltd., Belfast; 1945, 8,213gt, 474 feet
Eight-cylinder 2SCDA Burmeister & Wain-type oil engine by Harland and Wolff Ltd., Belfast

HUNTINGDON

Closely associated with the New Zealand Shipping Co. Ltd. was Federal Line, both companies becoming part of the P. & O. Group in 1916. Federal built some big cargo ships: perhaps not surprisingly, as their services to Australia and New Zealand took them half way round the world, and they had to endure the full fury of the southern oceans.

Huntingdon was one of Federal's biggest post war ships, part of a class shared with New Zealand Shipping. She had six hatches and, as this picture shows, a full outfit of masts, kingposts and derricks to serve them. Her career was long but uneventful, and in 1975 she was sold directly to breakers in Taiwan.

Alexander Stephen and Sons Ltd., Linthouse, Glasgow; 1948, 11,281gt, 561 feet

Two five-cylinder 2SCSA Doxford oil engines by Alexander Stephen and Sons Ltd., Linthouse, Glasgow driving twin screws

ENTON

Enton looked exactly like a Federal or New Zealand Line ship except for one detail: her funnel. Its colours were those of Birt, Potter and Hughes Ltd., a company named after the individuals who founded Federal Line in the 1890s. Internally, Enton differed from most Federal and New Zealand ships in not having refrigerated space, and carried cargo which did not need keeping cool on services between Europe and New Zealand and Australia.

In 1955 Enton was transferred to a new company, Avenue Shipping Co. Ltd. While part-owners Federal Line used names of English counties, Avenue named its ships after Irish counties, and Enton became Limerick. She continued running to the antipodes until 1969, when a transfer inside the P. & O. Group saw her become Howra of British India. In 1972 she was sold to Singapore owners who ran her successfully as Golden Haven until she was sold to breakers in Karachi in 1982.

Alexander Stephen and Sons Ltd., Linthouse, Glasgow; 1952, 6,443gt, 460 feet

Five-cylinder 2SCSA Doxford oil engine by Barclay, Curle and Co. Ltd., Glasgow

LOCH RYAN

Loch Ryan was one of the standard fast cargo liners built for the Government during the war. Her two steam turbines gave her a speed of 15 knots - a significant advance on the plodding 9 knots which was all that could be expected from the steam reciprocating engines of the more plentiful tramp-type standard ships. Names for this group were more carefully chosen than for other Empires, and *Empire Chieftain* was selected for this Tees-side built ship. As soon as she was put up for sale in 1946, Royal Mail bought her and renamed her *Loch Ryan*. They were to get a modest 14 years' service from her, and in 1960 she was sold to a Greek owner who wasted little effort when he changed her name from *Loch Ryan* to *Fair Ryan*. In common with many other ex-British ships, this sale was in order for her to make one last voyage, probably with a cargo of scrap metal. After this was delivered the ship itself went to a scrap yard at Nagasaki.

Furness Shipbuilding Co. Ltd., Haverton Hill-on-Tees; 1943, 9,904gt, 498 feet

Two steam turbines by Richardsons, Westgarth and Co. Ltd., Hartlepool driving a single screw

DRINA

Royal Mail's *Drina* had an unusual profile, because her forecastle was combined with her bridge deck and extended for 375 feet. She was designed for the River Plate meat trade which required big, insulated holds and refrigeration machinery to keep the carcasses frozen.

In the 1960s, the meat exporting countries of South America insisted that a greater proportion of their trade be carried in their own ships, and inevitably British lines had to accept an equivalent decline in trade. In 1965 and 1966, Royal Mail transferred *Drina* and her sister *Durango* to Shaw, Savill - another company within the Furness group. As *Romanic* and *Ruthenic*, respectively, they were put into the New Zealand meat trade but, as Shaw, Savill received new ships, they were withdrawn in 1967. *Romanic* was laid up at Belfast, and then sold and renamed *Sussex* for a last voyage out east to the breakers.
Harland and Wolff Ltd., Belfast; 1944, 9,785gt, 469 feet Two six-cylinder 2SCDA Burmeister & Wain-type oil engines by Harland and Wolff Ltd., Belfast driving twin screws

PARDO

The Royal Mail Steam Packet Company had a long and distinguished history, being one of the first companies set up to run ocean-going steamer services. Its ambitions were originally to run to the West Indies, China, Australia and the Pacific, but following the granting of a royal charter in 1839, it concentrated on the then very important trade with the West Indies. Eventually, routes expanded to include southern ports in the United States, much of South America, and as far north on the Pacific as Vancouver.

Although Royal Mail's passenger ships used ports in southern England, its cargo liners like *Pardo* were regular visitors to the Mersey, reflecting the importance of Liverpool and Manchester to the export trade. *Pardo* was the first of a group of eight motorships built for Royal Mail whose delivery coincided with the Second World War, and two of them were lost during that conflict. In 1964, four of the six survivors were sold en bloc to a Greek owner for £440,000, *Pardo* becoming *Aristarchos*. She gave her new owner just three years' service before being broken up in Taiwan during 1967.
Harland and Wolff Ltd., Belfast; 1940, 5,405gt, 450 feet Six-cylinder 2SCDA Burmeister & Wain-type oil engine by Harland and Wolff Ltd., Belfast

PORT VICTOR

Seen here, *Port Victor* looks like a normal cargo ship, but she had a very different appearance when completed. Whilst building she was taken over by the Admiralty who completed her as the aircraft carrier *HMS Nairana*. Known as 'Woolworth carriers', such conversions were cheap and quickly-built alternatives to the fully equipped fleet carriers, proving invaluable in defending convoys from U-boats and long-distance Focke Wolff Condors. After the war *HMS Nairana* was lent to the Royal Netherlands Navy and became *Karel Doorman*. In 1948 she was returned to the UK, and was rebuilt as originally intended as a cargo ship. Her career ended in July 1971 when she arrived at Faslane on the Clyde to be demolished.

Port Line ships were familiar on Merseyside, although the company was London based. It had its inception in a 1914 merger of four companies with interests in Australasian services. Although the merged company gave all its ship *Port* names, it retained the somewhat unwieldy title Commonwealth and Dominion Line Ltd. until 1937 when it became simply Port Line Ltd.

John Brown and Co. Ltd., Clydebank; 1943, 10,409gt, 529 feet
Two five-cylinder 2SCSA oil engines by John Brown and Co. Ltd., Clydebank driving a single screw

ROYSTON GRANGE

Houlder Line, whose ships served South America, had the rather endearing habit of giving its ships 'Grange' names which began with the individual letters of the words Houlder Brothers. It meant that names were used many times, and *Royston Grange* was carried by five ships, of which this was the third.

Houlder's major trade was bringing meat home from the River Plate, and for this they built big refrigerator ships. The third *Royston Grange* was not a typical Houlder reefer, but a rather basic standard ship built during wartime in Canada as *Fort Ash* (these ships are described further on page 55). Bought in 1948, she was something of a stopgap, and was quickly sold when more suitable tonnage could be completed.

From 1952 she had a succession of Italian and Greek owners, who named her *Guian*, *Cinqueterre*, *Tilemahos* and *Elios* before she was broken up during 1967 in what was then Yugoslavia.

Burrard Dry Dock Co. Ltd., Vancouver, British Columbia; 1943, 7,131gt, 442 feet
T. 3-cyl. by Dominion Engineering Works Ltd., Montreal

ST. ESSYLT

The owners of *St. Essylt*, George Bailey and Richard Street, had both formed tramp shipping companies in 1926, and they came together to create the B and S Shipping Co. Ltd. of Cardiff in 1933. The Government's Scrap and Build scheme enabled them to order three ships from Thompsons as the nucleus of a liner service to South America. By 1939 the title of the company had become the South American Saint Line Ltd. and it was offering sailings at ten-day intervals.

Sold in 1965, *St. Essylt* found a British buyer, the China Navigation Co. Ltd. who renamed her *Yunnan* and used her in the Far East. She was sold once more, to a Chinese owner who named her *Lucky Two*, and was broken up in Taiwan early in 1979.

Joseph L. Thompson and Sons Ltd., Sunderland; 1948, 6,855gt, 472 feet
Five-cylinder 2SCSA oil engine by William Doxford and Sons Ltd., Sunderland

DEERPOOL

Ropners were old-established north-east coast tramp shipowners, but had some innovations to their credit, including running their own shipyard, and investing in turbine-engined and diesel-driven tramps in the 1930s when most tramp owners were content to rely on steam reciprocating engines.

In 1946, Ropners began a liner service from Europe to the Gulf of Mexico, at the same time adopting an attractive, if unusual, green hull colour which *Deerpool* is wearing in this photograph. She was the second of two new ships built for the Gulf service and, like most contemporary cargo liners, had accommodation for a dozen passengers. Alas, she was not to last long in the fleet, and in 1961 was sold to Yugoslavia who got another 11 years' service out of her as *Kordun* before demolishing her at Split in 1972.

Sir James Laing and Sons Ltd., Sunderland; 1950, 5,169gt, 445 feet
Four-cylinder 4SCSA Doxford-type oil engine by R. and W. Hawthorn, Leslie and Co. Ltd., Newcastle-upon-Tyne

EMPIRE DOVE

In 1945 the victorious Allies took not only what little of the German fleet was left afloat following intensive bombing of German ports, but also ships which were still under construction. Laid down in Holland during 1940, this ship was to be named *Hermes* but was completed in Germany. Work progressed very slowly, due to shortages of materials, bomb damage, and Allied restrictions on German industry. Eventually, in 1949, nine years after being started, the ship came to the UK as *Empire Dove*.

She was intended for short-sea services and was quickly put onto routes to Spain and Portugal, in 1953 becoming *Pozarica* for MacAndrews - a British company which was to build most of its future ships in Germany. *Pozarica* was sold to Spanish owners in 1964 and renamed *Blue Fin*. On 27th November 1965 she lost her rudder in heavy weather in the Bay of Biscay and sank the next day. She was on a voyage from Antwerp to Barcelona.

N.V. Scheepswerven Gebroeder Pot, Bolnes, Holland; 1949, 2,503gt, 360 feet
Five-cylinder 2SCDA oil engine by Bremer Vulkan, Vegesack, Germany

PINTO

Fruit from Spain and Portugal was the staple import that kept the smart little motor ships of MacAndrews and Co. Ltd. running. Their major trade was into the Thames, but they also made fortnightly sailings from Liverpool. *Pinto* and her sisters were small but carefully designed, as they needed to get into the smaller ports on the Iberian Peninsula, and had to brave the storms of the Bay of Biscay.

Pinto was sold to a small Greek shipowner in 1965, and as *Panaghia P* she tramped round Europe from the Mediterranean to the Baltic. In May 1978 she arrived at a shipbreaking yard in Vigo, a Spanish port she would have visited many times in a long career.

William Doxford and Sons Ltd., Sunderland; 1947, 2,579gt, 352 feet
Five-cylinder 2SCSA oil engine by William Doxford and Sons Ltd., Sunderland

PINZON

Pinzon and her sister *Pizarro* were slight oddities in MacAndrews' fleet, as few fruiters of this period had their engines aft. They were advanced for 1922-built ships in having diesel engines, as the first ocean-going motorship had been completed only a decade earlier. The choice of diesel machinery helped them achieve the shallow draft which gave them access to a wide range of Spanish and Portuguese harbours.

Pizarro was a war loss, torpedoed by an Italian submarine in January 1941, but *Pinzon* motored on until 1951 when she was sold to Finnish owners as *Havny*. At the end of 1960 she was reported as idle at Brussels, and in February 1961 she was sold for demolition.

William Beardmore and Co. Ltd., Glasgow; 1922, 1,365gt, 241 feet
Six-cylinder 4SCSA oil engine by William Beardmore and Co. Ltd., Glasgow

ORSOVA

Just occasionally, a big passenger liner not normally seen on the Mersey came to take advantage of Liverpool's large dry docks. Hence, Basil Feilden would have been pleased to catch the *Orsova*, probably coming from her builders at Barrow-in-Furness to be drydocked before entering service.

Orsova belonged to the Orient Steam Navigation Co. Ltd. who maintained a service from London to Sydney which, before the coming of reliable and fast air travel, was undoubtedly the preferred way to reach Australia. *Orsova's* owners were part of P.&O., but wisely they kept the Orient Line branding, with the ship's distinctive styling and corn-coloured hull. Regrettably, in 1964 new managers took management consultants' advice and bundled all its shipowning under the P.&O. umbrella.

Sadly, but inevitably, air travel made a month's sea voyage to Australia seem wildly extravagant of time, and the old Orient Line service was abandoned. In spite of the burgeoning cruise market, no-one wanted *Orsova* and on 14th February 1974 she arrived at Kaohsiung to be broken up. *Vickers-Armstrongs Ltd., Barrow-in-Furness; 1954, 28,790gt, 723 feet Six steam turbines by Vickers-Armstrongs Ltd., Barrow-in-Furness driving twin screws*

43

WAYNEGATE

For a small port, Whitby produced a remarkable number of tramp shipowners in the nineteenth century. Probably the most successful company to have its origins in the North Yorkshire town - and certainly the one that survived longest - was Turnbull, Scott and Company. Although the company moved to London in 1869, its connections with Whitby were maintained by naming its ships after streets and other landmarks in and around the town.

Waynegate was a wartime standard ship of the C type, similar to *Hesperides* on page 25. She was actually completed for the Admiralty as the submarine maintenance ship *HMS Mullion Cove*, but was converted to a cargo ship in 1948 when she became *Margaret Clunies*. Turnbull, Scott bought her in 1951 and kept her for ten years as *Waynegate*. After they sold her, she ran as *Katingo, President Magsaysay* and then simply *Magsaysay*. After a fire in July 1968 when she was bound from the Philippines to Korea, she was fit only for scrap, and Korean breakers finished her off.

Bartram and Sons Ltd., Sunderland; 1944, 7,416gt, 431 feet
T. 3-cyl. by Duncan Stewart and Co. Ltd., Glasgow

RUNSWICK

Another long-lived Whitby owner, Headlam and Son, remained true to their home, registering their ships in Whitby right until the end. *Runswick* was in truth a rather old-fashioned tramp, retaining coal-fired boilers. Her hull is notable as being of the long-bridge-deck type, much favoured by Whitby owners and others in the north east of England.

Although sold in 1955, the ship went on to have a long career, first as *San Salvador* and then as *Eugenio,* as which she was at last converted to oil burning in 1962. She was broken up in Spain in 1971.

J.L. Thompson and Sons Ltd., Sunderland; 1930, 4,024gt, 379 feet
C. 4-cyl. by J. Dickinson and Sons Ltd., Sunderland

ARGODON

Greek shipowners did not get where they are today by sitting and dreaming on their islands. A significant number left Greece, most notably to settle in London where much of the world's maritime business was done. One such was A. Lusi, the ultimate owner of the *Argodon*. She had been built as the *Fort Nakasley*.

As the post-war boom blew itself out in the mid-1950s, it became less profitable to own ageing tramps under the British flag, and many of the London Greeks moved their tonnage to flags of convenience - cheaper and less well regulated - or simply sold them. In 1956 *Argodon* was sold to become *Union Metropole*, owned by China Union Lines Ltd. of Hong Kong. She arrived at Kaohsiung to be broken up late in 1967.

West Coast Shipbuilders Ltd., Vancouver, British Columbia; 1943, 7,106gt, 440 feet
T. 3-cyl. by John Inglis Co. Ltd., Toronto

PETFRANO

Although we feature a number of Canadian- and US-built war standard ships, we have not forgotten the ships built during the Second World War in British yards. Their output, although by no means matching that of the US, was substantial and varied, reflecting the need for vessels as diverse as tankers to bring in fuel and tugs to rescue damaged ships.

The steamer shown here was one of the numerous type of British standard freighters, the B type. Built as *Empire Carpenter*, in 1944 she was loaned to the USSR as *Dickson*. Although by no means all such ships were given back - the US eventually gave up on a number of Liberties lent to our Russian allies - *Dickson* was returned in 1946.

In 1947 she was sold to an owner from Yugoslavia in exile in London, and registered as *Petfrano* under the name of the Petrinovic Steamship Co. Ltd. In 1955, she went to Greek owners, first as *Amipa*, then as *Apex* and finally *Afros*, being broken up in Shanghai during 1971.

Charles Connell and Co. Ltd., Glasgow; 1943, 6,995gt, 446 feet
T. 3-cyl. by David Rowan and Co. Ltd., Glasgow

SEA MINSTREL

Other examples of the British wartime output were the modest-sized ships known as the Scandinavian type. Their derrick posts were placed at the ends of the holds to give the maximum room for deck cargoes. Perfected by owners and yards in Scandinavia, this design was originally developed for the Baltic timber trade, where logs and sawn timbers were loaded on deck once the hatches were filled. In wartime such a rig proved useful for maximising deck space for loads of military equipment. *Vianna* on page 23 is a Canadian-built example of this type.

Completed as *Empire Elgar* - one of 25 ships of this type built and engined at West Hartlepool - she was purchased in 1947 by the London-based Dover Navigation Co. Ltd. to become *Sea Minstrel*. Sold on after only four years she went first to owners in Newcastle-upon-Tyne as *Marandellas*, then to a Norwegian owners who renamed her first *Edward Jansen* and later *Slitan*, and finally to the Bulgarian state merchant fleet as *Pirin*. In 1965 she was broken up at Split in Yugoslavia.
William Gray and Co. Ltd., West Hartlepool; 1942, 2,847gt, 328 feet
T. 3-cyl. by Central Marine Engine Works, West Hartlepool

REYNOLDS

Some tramps were built with a view to chartering to liner companies because such companies occasionally suffered severe shortages of tonnage. A classic example was during the Suez crisis when, with the canal closed, ships had to steam round the Cape of Good Hope, considerably lengthening voyages. The answer was to charter good quality tonnage from tramp owners and, during such periods of high demand, ships like the *Reynolds* of the Bolton Steam Shipping Co. Ltd., London would often make excellent money.

In 1961 *Reynolds* actually became a full time liner, although not under the Red Ensign. She was sold to Pakistan owners, who renamed here *Imtiazbaksh*. As this she continued to visit the Mersey, but now on a regular liner service which berthed in the docks on the Birkenhead side of the river. *Imtiazbaksh* was broken up in Pakistan during 1976.

William Pickersgill and Sons Ltd., Sunderland; 1953, 6,247gt, 458 feet
T. 3-cyl. with low pressure turbine by North Eastern Marine Engineering Co. (1938) Ltd., Sunderland

LIGURIA

When Basil Feilden photographed the *Liguria* in 1950, she would have been an unusual visitor to the Mersey. Basically an emigrant ship, with holds fitted with dormitory-style accommodation for over 900 passengers, she had been chartered to make trans-Atlantic voyages with students during the Roman Catholic Holy Year. Not a large vessel, the lifeboats needed for her complement had to be double-banked. Neither was *Liguria* a fast ship, Atlantic crossings taking ten days each way.

She had been built as the *Hilda Woermann* for service between Germany and East Africa, but the First World War dealt a death blow to this trade, and she was taken over by Australian owners who ran her to Singapore as *Marella*. Her emigrant career started after the Second World War, with Italian owners, first as *Captain Marcos,* then as *Liguria* and finally as *Corsica*. A combination of mechanical failures and the mounting debt of her owners (they often go together) led to the *Corsica* being laid up in 1952 and scrapped in Belgium in 1954.

Reiherstieg Schiffswerf und Maschine Fabriek, Hamburg, Germany; 1914, 7,475gt, 442 feet

Q.8-cyl. by Reiherstieg Schiffswerf und Maschine Fabriek, Hamburg, Germany driving twin screws

SYDNEY

Photographed by Basil Feilden when she had called at Liverpool during a series of emigrant voyages to Quebec, the appearance of the *Sydney* totally belies her wartime role as an aircraft carrier. US built, on a hull intended to be a cargo ship, as *HMS Fencer* she had a particularly good war, escorting convoys and hunting submarines. Her aircraft sank at least four U-boats.

In 1950 she was sold to Achille Lauro of Naples and heavily rebuilt in Genoa as seen here, to carry a total of 758 passengers between Italy and Australia. When the Australian service succumbed to aircraft competition, she was renamed *Roma* in 1968 and sent cruising. After Achille Lauro sold her in 1970 her career deteriorated into a dismal round of renamings, machinery breakdowns and arrests as various unhappy owners tried to continue her cruising career as *Galaxy Queen*, *Lady Tina*, and *Caribia 2*. She was scrapped in 1974 at La Spezia.

Western Pipe and Steel Co., San Francisco, California, USA; 1944, 14,708gt, 492 feet
Two steam turbines by General Electric Company, Lynn, Massachusetts, USA driving a single screw

HMS CAMPANIA

The 1951 Festival of Britain was centred on London, but the organisers at least made a valiant effort to take some of its attractions to the public outside the capital. The vehicle chosen to display the exhibits around the coast was the hull of an aircraft carrier, of which there were plenty spare at the end of the war.

Like two other conversions featured in this album, *HMS Campania* began life as a mercantile hull - ordered by Shaw, Savill and Albion. Delivered in 1944, she was surplus to requirements once peace broke out, because the Navy preferred its purpose-built fleet carriers. After service as an exhibition ship, *HMS Campania* was demolished at Blyth late in 1955. Note the coal-fired tug belonging to the Furness Group in the foreground of Basil Feilden's photograph.

Harland and Wolff Ltd., Belfast; 1944, 12,450 tons displacement, 540 feet
Two oil engines by Harland and Wolff Ltd., Belfast driving twin screws

GEORGE L. DUVAL

George L. Duval was one of the Liberty types which materially assisted the Allies to win the Second World War. With the Battle of the Atlantic not going well, and an obvious need to ship US armed forces to theatres of war in Europe, Africa and the Pacific, a shipbuilding programme was begun to which the term 'massive' can hardly do justice. A staggering 2,710 Liberties were built, mostly in newly created shipyards and often by workers recruited to these yards who had never before seen the sea, never mind a ship.

Not surprisingly, this massive fleet could not all be employed in peacetime, and most Liberties were soon laid up. But then it was said during the war that, if a Liberty made only one voyage, it had done its job. Less than half were ever to see further service, and the subject of this photograph, built as *Fred E. Joyce*, was idle at Wilmington from 1947 until 1951 when bought by Wessel Duval and Co. Inc. of New York and renamed *George L. Duval*. Later names carried were *National Freedom*, *Valiant Freedom* and *Mount Hood* - all for US owners who operated the ship under various flags. She was broken up in Japan during 1961.
New England Shipbuilding Corporation, Portland, Maine, USA; 1945; 7,255gt, 442 feet
T. 3-cyl. by General Machinery Corporation, Hamilton, Ontario

SAN JORGE

The United States was initially reluctant to sell its many surplus Liberties to foreign owners, afraid that with their lower operating costs they would undercut US lines. But it was soon realised that these nine-knot ships were best suited to tramping, and did not offer serious competition to US owners who specialised in liners.

British and Greek owners were the principal beneficiaries of Liberty sales. The *San Jorge* was acquired by the Greek Lyras family in January 1948, and although she changed registered owners, flags, management offices and names several times (becoming *Saint John* in 1954), it was the Lyras family which sold her for scrap in mainland China at the end of 1967.

She had been built as *Andres Almonaster*, and served the US Navy briefly as *Syrma*.
Delta Shipbuilding Co. Inc., New Orleans, USA; 1944, 7,176gt, 442 feet
T. 3-cyl. by the American Shipbuilding Co., Cleveland, Ohio, USA

GREEN MOUNTAIN STATE

By 1943, the United States had proved that it could construct ships in the vast numbers needed to wage a global war: in that year alone it was scheduled to deliver no fewer than 1,200 Liberties. Two factors led the US to change course and start building more sophisticated freighters. The first was knowledge that the British were planning to build a fast cargo liner type. The second influence was that shipbuilding capability was running ahead of steel production so, rather than build a 9-knot Liberty, it was better to use the available steel to build a 15-knot ship which could sail free of convoy and had the speed to give the military significant operational advantages. Hence the advent of the turbine-driven Victory type.

Green Mountain State had been *Flagstaff Victory* until 1949 when she had been bought by States Marine Corporation. Although less numerous than the Liberties, Victories featured in a number of post-war cargo liner fleets, including those of Blue Funnel, Furness Withy, and Donaldson Line, whilst others were in Dutch, Belgian, Indian, Argentine and South African ownership.

Green Mountain State was given one more name, *Reliance Solidarity*, before being broken up at Kaohsiung in 1971.
California Shipbuilding Corporation; Los Angeles, California, USA; 1945, 7,641gt, 455 feet
Two steam turbines by General Electric Company, Lynn, Massachusetts, USA driving a single screw

SUE LYKES

Ships belonging to Lykes Line of New Orleans were familiar in the Mersey, often bringing cotton from the southern states of the USA. Like most United States fleets in the 1950s, it was made up entirely of wartime standard ships.

Sue Lykes was a C2 type, intended to be named *Tornado*. The C2 type was actually designed before the war, with the intention of giving the US fast, effective merchant ships for national defence as well as meeting the needs of its coastal and deep-sea shipowners.

After a long life, *Sue Lykes* was scrapped in Taiwan during 1972. With the passing of this generation of ships, US companies faced a major problem because, by law, all US-registered ships had to be built in the USA and manned there, and both these stipulations were becoming prohibitively expensive. Lykes Lines are one of the few US companies to have survived - at least in name - into the new millennium, although the few ships with Lykes names are now part of the American President Line, itself a subsidiary of a Singapore company.

North Carolina Shipbuilding Co., Wilmington, North Carolina, USA; 1945, 8,295gt, 441 feet

Two steam turbines by General Electric Co., Lynn, Massachusetts, USA driving a single screw

AMERICAN SCOUT

The US emergency shipbuilding programme did not cease with the end of the Second World War, but continued building ships which US operators could trade in post-war years. *American Scout* was built for United States Lines, a company formed with government help not long after the First World War. They continued running services across the Atlantic with ships carrying *American* names, and across the Pacific where names beginning *Pioneer* were favoured. On his visits to Eastham, Basil Feilden would have noticed United States Lines' distinctive red, white and blue funnels parked by the masting crane whilst the ships went up the Ship Canal to Manchester.

American Scout was sold in 1971 to become *Interscout*, trading in the Far East. But her subsequent career was short: in October 1971 the grain cargo she was lightering from a tanker in Chittagong Roads shifted, and she rolled over and had to be broken up.

North Carolina Shipbuilding Co., Wilmington, North Carolina, USA; 1946, 8,295gt, 441 feet
Two steam turbines by General Electric Co., Lynn, Massachusetts, USA driving a single screw

SOUTHWIND

Southwind was basically similar to *Sue Lykes* and *American Scout*, but there were many variations amongst the C2 types, affecting mainly the cargo gear. *Southwind* had been completed as an attack cargo ship for the US Navy under the name *Caswell*, well-armed and fitted with lattice masts in naval style. When fitted with more conventional masts after the war, she had a subtly different appearance to near-sisters such as *American Scout*.

The C2s formed the backbone of many US commercial fleets in the 1950s, *Southwind* going to the South Atlantic Steamship Line Inc. of Savannah, Georgia. In 1961 she returned to the US Government ownership as *American Surveyor* and was laid up on the James River as part of the vast reserve fleet intended to avoid the need for another emergency shipbuilding programme. She was taken out of reserve and scrapped in Philadelphia during 1974.

North Carolina Shipbuilding Co., Wilmington, North Carolina, USA; 1944, 8,295gt, 441 feet
Two steam turbines by General Electric Co., Lynn, Massachusetts, USA driving a single screw

TAR HEEL MARINER

With their immense wartime building programme, one would have thought that the United States had sufficient ships to last out the century. But no. With the outbreak of the Korean War in 1950, the US Government agreed to a further building programme of fast freighters with military potential, the Mariner class.

Naming seemed a problem; names of most famous Americans (and many not so famous) had already been used for the Liberties. The solution was to give Mariners the nicknames of various States plus the suffix *Mariner.* It was all very patriotic but lacking in dignity when the result was *Tar Heel Mariner.* She was registered in the port of Wilmington, in the state of North Carolina.

When Basil Feilden photographed her, *Tar Heel Mariner* was on charter to Pacific Far East Lines Inc. of San Francisco, whose title suggests the ship was not running on her normal service, but bringing military supplies to the UK. This company later bought her and renamed her *Washington Bear.* Finishing her career under the name *John B. Waterman*, she was broken up in Taiwan during 1980.
Newport News Shipbuilding and Drydock Co., Newport News, Virginia, USA; 1952, 9,215gt, 530 feet Two steam turbines by General Electric Co., Lynn, Massachusetts, USA driving a single screw

SHOW ME MARINER

None of the Mariners were complete before the end of the Korean conflict, and most were sold or chartered to commercial operators who found these big 20-knot ships useful if expensive to run.

Basil Feilden was lucky to get a photograph of *Show Me Mariner*, as she was completed in January 1954 but in September of that year was placed in the reserve fleet on the James River along with hundreds of ageing Liberties. In 1956, she was sold to United States Lines for their Pacific services as *Pioneer Mill.* Her life was extended by conversion to the containership *American Alliance* in 1969, and she survived until 1987 when broken up in Kaohsiung.
Bethlehem Steel Co., Shipbuilding Division, Sparrows Point, Maryland, USA; 1954, 9,212gt, 530 feet Two steam turbines by Bethlehem Steel Co. Shipbuilding Division, Quincy, Massachusetts, USA driving a single screw

RONDEAU PARK

Unable to build ships as fast as the wolf packs of German U-boats could sink them, the British Government turned to Canada with a plea for help in the early years of the Second World War. Canada's tiny shipbuilding industry responded magnificently, expanding to the extent of building not only 450 merchant ships but also some 300 warships. Freighters such as *Rondeau Park* made a major contribution to the hard-fought Battle of the Atlantic, helping to ensure the eventual Allied victory.

After the war, *Rondeau Park* was sold to London-based Greek owners and became the *Sycamore Hill* of Counties Ship Management Ltd. She was broken up at Hong Kong in 1966.
United Shipyards Ltd., Montreal; 1944, 7,138gt, 441 feet
T. 3-cyl. by Dominion Engineering Works Ltd., Montreal

FORT STURGEON

Although there was no discernible difference between the Forts and the Parks, the Canadian ships were built under these two separate naming schemes. They were constructed to a design worked out in Sunderland, that of *Empire Liberty*, whose drawings also formed the basis of the US-built Liberty type (see page 50), and the B type standard ship built in the UK during the war (see *Petfrano* on page 45). One of the pieces of minutiae beloved of enthusiasts was that the Forts and Parks could be told apart from the B type at a distance because the latter had a much bigger gap between the funnel and the derrick posts serving the third hatch.

Fort Sturgeon joined the *Rondeau Park* in the fleet of Counties Ship Management Ltd. as *East Hill*, but in 1957 was sold on to become *Rio Alto* and in 1965 became *Aktor*. Her life as *Aktor* was short: on 1st June 1966 she foundered in the Pacific about 800 miles off California after springing a leak in heavy weather. Her cargo was sugar from Cuba to China.
Victoria Machinery Depot Co. Ltd., Victoria, British Columbia; 1943, 7,127gt, 441 feet
T. 3-cyl. by Canadian Allis-Chalmers Ltd., Montreal

SVANHOLM

The elderly but well-kept steamer *Svanholm* operated on the DFDS route from the Baltic ports including Copenhagen to Liverpool, Manchester and Swansea. Note her name painted amidships, almost a trademark of Danish companies. After becoming too old for DFDS liner services, *Svanholm* was used by the company as a tramp for a few years before being laid up in 1957 and broken up in Belgium during 1960.

DFDS - the United Shipping Company - for many years operated a network of regular liner services centred on Copenhagen. But unlike many British companies who ran similar networks, DFDS have survived the era of containerisation and roll-on, roll-off vehicle ferries, and are still a major force in European shipping with important routes on the North Sea and Baltic, although their ships no longer serve the Mersey.

Helsingørs Jernskibs-og Maskinbyggeri, Elsinore, Denmark; 1922, 1,321gt, 260 feet
T. 3-cyl. by Helsingørs Jernskibs-og Maskinbyggeri, Elsinore, Denmark

SILJA DAN

Many of the ships of Danish owner J. Lauritzen were specially ice strengthened for service in polar waters. Some of these vessels, notably *Magga Dan* and *Kista Dan*, became very well known for their work with polar expeditions in the 1950s.

Silja Dan was built for the Finnish trade, and was in original condition when photographed by Basil Feilden leaving Eastham Locks. Later she was modified to run in Arctic conditions when Lauritzens won a contract to carry lead ore from Mestersvig in Greenland.

Silja Dan was sold in 1964 and renamed *Veli* by owners who traded her from Finnish ports as originally intended. On 22nd January 1971 she was abandoned by her crew in the Gulf of Bothnia when fire broke out in the engine room soon after leaving Hamina for Barrow-in-Furness. She was towed into Rauma and the fire put out, but at 20 years old there was little point in repairing her, and she was broken up at Helsinki.

Aalborg Vaerft A/S, Aalborg, Denmark; 1951, 3,588gt, 321 feet
C. 3-cyl. by Maskinfabrikken Atlas A/S, Copenhagen, Denmark

CRESCO

One of the joys of watching ships on the Mersey is that almost anything can turn up. *Cresco* looks an unremarkable, if elderly, small freighter but delving into her history reveals - as so often - something of interest.

She was built as *Cresco* in neutral Holland during the First World War for owners in Norway, which was also neutral. With British builders working flat out to replace war losses, Dutch ships and yards did very nicely, thank you, during the war, and were accused of working for both sides. Although *Cresco* was delivered to Norway, she was soon taken over by the British, who were hard pressed for tonnage, in an act of doubtful legality considering we were not at war with Norway. Often some spurious pretext - like carrying coal mined in German-occupied Belgian - was used to justify such high-handed actions.

Cresco went back to her rightful owners in 1919, and when Basil Feilden took this photograph in the early 1950s she was still in Norwegian hands, owned by E.B. Aabys Rederi A/S of Oslo. After spending her last three years under the German flag as *Wittorf*, she was broken up at Hamburg in 1958.

Huiskens and van Dyk, Dordrecht, Holland; 1916, 1,297gt, 238 feet
T. 3-cyl. by Huiskens and van Dyk, Dordrecht, Holland

CHRISTEN SMITH

In the 1920s, Norway's Christen Smith introduced a new concept to shipping. With individual items of cargo such as railway locomotives and rolling stock getting bigger and heavier, Christen Smith saw a market for vessels which could not only carry such items as deck cargo, but also lift them on and off with their own gear. With the help of British shipbuilders, he developed the heavy-lift ship which had long clear deck areas and massive masts and derricks.

Named as a tribute to the founder, the *Christen Smith* was a later example of the breed although, somewhat surprisingly for a Scandinavian ship, she was built as a steamer. She gave good service, although her rebuilding with a diesel engine in 1958 would have been expensive. Renamed *Belforest* she lasted in the fleet until 1972. Greek owners got a few more years service from her as *Marigo,* and after two years in lay up at Piraeus she was broken up in Spain in 1979.

Although indivisible items of cargo have got even heavier, and now include chemical plant and entire container cranes, Christen Smith's company has now left the development of heavy-lift ships to others and has concentrated instead on standard bulk carriers.

Fredrikstad M/V A/B., Fredrikstad, Norway; 1947, 5,229gt, 418 feet
C. 4-cyl. by Fredrikstad M/V A/B., Fredrikstad, Norway

VENTURA

To become a total loss once is unfortunate, but this Norwegian motorship achieved the feat twice within little more than two years.

Ventura's early life was peaceful enough. She was built for Halfdan Ditlev-Simonsen and Co. of Oslo, in whose colours she is seen here. In 1965 she changed hands within Norway, becoming Martin Bakke, and in 1971 found her third Norwegian owner who named her Rytterholm.

On 27th September 1974 she ran aground at Tsamkong whilst bringing in a cargo of fertiliser. Although her insurers decided the cost of repairs exceeded her value and declared her a constructive total loss, her owner decided it was worth returning her to service. But on 12th October 1976 she was carrying more fertiliser, this time from Porsgrunn to Bangkok, when her cargo shifted in heavy weather and she foundered trying to enter Corunna Bay. This time there was no reprieve.

Kockums M/V A/B, Malmo, Sweden; 1951, 5,713gt, 462 feet

Six-cylinder 2SCDA oil engine by Kockums M/V A/B, Malmo, Sweden

PATRIA

Poor Finland was a curious victim of the Second World War. She was already fighting for her life against the USSR, when her giant neighbour woke up to the reality of German aggression in 1941. Once the USSR became one of the Allies, Finland was defined as an enemy. The steamer Patria was a minor result of this situation, as she was ordered from Finland during the war by the German Navy.

The Finnish yard completed her after the war, and sold her to Finland Steamship Co. Ltd., the country's largest shipping line. For twenty years she ran on regular routes, like that between Finland and Manchester on which Basil Feilden photographed her just after leaving Eastham Locks. In 1967 she was sold to an Italian owner who traded her as Galatea before selling her for scrap sometime in the late 1970s.

Wartsila-Koncernen A/B Crichton-Vulcan, Abo, Finland; 1947, 2,162, 281 feet

C. 4-cyl. Christiansen & Meyer steam engine by Wartsila-Koncernen A/B Crichton-Vulcan, Abo, Finland

STAD ALKMAAR

Owners of Dutch coasters had been using diesel engines since the 1920s, with dramatic results in terms of fuel economy and maximising cargo space. It is surprising, therefore, to find that Halcyon-Lijn N.V. of Rotterdam were specifying steam engines for their tramp ships in post-war years. *Stad Alkmaar* had an old-fashioned three-cylinder triple-expansion engine, the only concession to modernity being a low pressure turbine fitted to get any residual energy out of the steam once it had been through the three cylinders. In layout she was like many contemporary British

tramps, but *Stad Alkmaar* had a mast just ahead of the funnel, in a position where a pair of derrick posts would be more usual.

In 1965 *Stad Alkmaar* was sold to Italian owners as *Lamone* and, despite her obsolescent machinery, lasted until 1973 when she was broken up at Ravenna.

N.V. Mch. & Scheepswerf van P. Smit junior, Rotterdam, Holland; 1948, 5,688gt, 474 feet

T. 3-cyl. with low-pressure turbine by N.V. Mch. & Scheepswerf van P. Smit junior, Rotterdam, Holland

FOO YU

During the First World War, Japan saw the world demanding ships at almost any price and began building sizeable steamers. The British Government was desperate for tonnage and took some, but many more went to build up Japanese fleets. Nippon Yusen Kaisha - the Japan Mail Steamship Co. - took delivery of this steamer as *Toba Maru*.

During the Second World War she was lost to Japan, when the US Navy and Air Forces achieved what the German submarines and aircraft had failed to do to the UK: cut off the island nation's communications by sinking almost all her merchant ships. *Toba Maru* was heavily damaged in an air attack on Keelung on the island of Taiwan in June 1945. After the war, when Taiwan was the only part of China not to become communist, she became *Tai Nan* and then *Foo Yu*. When Basil Feilden caught her in Liverpool, thousands of miles from home, *Foo Yu* was owned by the E-Hsiang Steam Ship Co. Ltd., of Taipeh. She was broken up in Taiwan in 1958. Note her unusual topmasts and the lattice-work derricks.

Kawasaki Dockyard Co. Ltd., Kobe, Japan; 1916, 6,995gt, 445 feet
T. 3-cyl by Kawasaki Dockyard Co. Ltd., Kobe, Japan

NACHIHARU MARU

The Japanese merchant fleet was almost totally destroyed during the Pacific War. This was a major factor in the Allied victory, as a shortage of ships meant the Japanese were unable to supply the garrisons they had established during their meteoric progress early in the war. It was estimated that in 1945 Japan had less than twenty deep-sea ships.

Although the occupiers kept Japanese industry under tight control for a few years, the US soon recognised that it was in its interests to allow the Japanese economy to grow again. Not only did it want to avoid having to continue to feed much of the population, but Japan's anti-communist attitude made it an excellent ally during the Cold War, and it was an important staging post for the Korean conflict. Rebuilding the merchant fleet was a priority, and one of the early products was the motor ship *Nachiharu Maru* of Shinnihon Kisen K.K. She must have been one of the first post-war Japanese ships Basil Feilden photographed.

In 1970 the *Nachiharu Maru* was sold to become *Prosperous City*, flying the Liberian flag but with a name suggesting Far Eastern ownership. She was broken up in Taiwan during 1972.

Hitachi Zosen K.K., Habu, Japan; 1951, 7,086, 439 feet
Six-cylinder 2SCSA oil engine by Hitachi Zosen K.K., Osaka, Japan

GRANNY SUZANNE

Did the Greek Tsavliris family have a special affection for the elderly lady after whom this ship is named? They have used the name *Granny Suzanne* repeatedly, mainly for elderly ships often on their final voyage to the breakers. This particular *Granny Suzanne* had an interesting history, having being built as *Iron Chief* to carry ore, limestone and coke on the Australian coast for the country's iron and steel industry. Replaced by a larger vessel in 1935, she returned to the UK where she had been built, surviving the war as Ropners' *Stagpool*.

The Tsavliris family bought her in 1950, registering her as *Granny*

Suzanne under the ownership of the Heron Steamship Co. Ltd. (Tsavliris (Shipping) Ltd., managers), London. Sold again in 1954, her new owner was based in a comfortable lakeside town in Switzerland, but chose to register his ship, now renamed *Carmen*, first under the Costa Rican and then the Panama flag. Her fate is a reminder that, even in the days of radar and other aids to navigation, marine accidents still happen. On 13th June 1963 *Carmen* sank after colliding with the Turkish steamer *Sadikzade* off the South Foreland. Two members of her crew were lost.

William Doxford and Sons Ltd., Sunderland; 1930, 4,549gt, 370 feet
T. 3-cyl. by George Clark Ltd., Sunderland

STAR OF ALEXANDRIA

Egypt has long had a modest merchant fleet. Before the Second World War its Khedivial Mail Line was taken back into Egyptian ownership after some years of poor management from Britain, and regained some of the prestige of its passenger services. More interested in cargo shipping was the Alexandria Navigation Co. S.A.E., founded in the 1930s. Its modest fleet was rebuilt after the war with ships such as *Star of Alexandria*.

The spate of nationalisation which saw the Suez Canal taken into state ownership also saw Egypt's private shipping companies coming under Government control from 1959. Subsequent owners of *Star of Alexandria* were the United Arab Maritime Company, reflecting Egypt's short-lived union with Syria as the United Arab Republic, which quickly became a disunited Arab republic as the two countries fell out with each other.

Star of Alexandria came to a dramatic and premature end, destroyed by sabotage in the continuing unrest in the Middle East. On 23rd July 1964 she was literally blown apart in the Algerian port of Annaba when a time bomb set off an explosion in her cargo of ammunition.
Cantieri Riuniti Dell'Adriatico, Trieste, Italy; 1953, 2,738gt, 349 feet
Six-cylinder 2SCSA oil engine by Cantieri Riuniti Dell'Adriatico, Trieste, Italy

STAR OF LUXOR

Relations between Egypt and Britain have not always been particularly friendly. During the Second World War, Britain's interest in the Suez Canal meant that Egypt - an independent country - was effectively used as a military base. And, of course, nationalisation of the Canal in 1956 and the subsequent ill-starred invasion did nothing to improve matters. Perhaps not surprisingly, Egypt did not look to British yards for new ships after the war, and the Alexandria Navigation Co. S.A.E. had *Star of Luxor* and *Star of Alexandria* built in Italy.

Star of Luxor enjoyed a long life, although latterly she was probably idle at Alexandria. In 1981 she was advertised for sale, and was briefly renamed *Star of Luxor II* and *Afriquia*, the latter probably only for her final voyage to the breakers in Split, Yugoslavia during 1983.

Cantieri Riuniti Dell'Adriatico, Trieste, Italy; 1948, 6,433gt, 408 feet
Six-cylinder 2SCSA oil engine by Cantieri Riuniti Dell'Adriatico, Trieste, Italy

ETROG

Few emergent nations had such an urgent need for ships as Israel, surrounded as she was by actively antagonistic Arab nations. As well as buying some secondhand ships, the state shipping line, Zim Israel Navigation Co. Ltd., acquired ships that were already building. One such was *Etrog,* which was nearing completion in a Swedish yard having been launched as *Carlshamn.*

Once established, Zim Israel pursued a policy of continuously updating its fleet, and *Etrog* was sold in 1961 to become *Leora* for another Israeli company. In 1968 she became the Panama-registered *Brothers,* and then *Sitia* in 1973. But on 17th December 1973 she was wrecked off Gaza.

Ekensberg Varv., Stockholm, Sweden; 1950, 1,845gt, 313 feet
Two seven-cylinder 4SCSA oil engines by Maschinenbau Augsburg-Nurnberg, Augsburg, Germany driving a single screw - new in 1954

MONA'S QUEEN

Seen racing for the landing stage, *Mona's Queen* was the second of six turbine passenger steamers built for the Isle of Man Steam Packet Co. Ltd. at Birkenhead in post-war years, the popularity of holidays in the Isle of Man keeping them all busy until the 1960s. The end of the Manx career of *Mona's Queens* was precipitated by the closure of sailings between Douglas and Fleetwood, where the berth had been declared unsafe. In 1962, at just 16 years of age, she was sold to Greek owners who were developing the Mediterranean cruising trade with relatively small ships. The Chandris Group, now owners of some of the largest cruise vessels, ran her under the names *Barrow Queen, Carissima, Carina* and *Fiesta*. She last cruised in 1974, and after a long lay up at Piraeus was broken up in 1981.

To understand why today's Mersey is much quieter than it was in Basil Feilden's time, we need only look at the size of fleets like that of the Isle of Man Steam Packet Co. Ltd. In 1953 it had 12 vessels, including nine passenger ships, many of which would be seen in Liverpool on a summer's day. Today the company has just one vehicle ferry and one fast ferry, the latter an unreliable performer in the bad weather not uncommon on the Irish Sea.
Cammell, Laird and Co. Ltd., Birkenhead; 1946, 2,485gt, 345 feet
Four steam turbines by Cammell, Laird and Co. Ltd., Birkenhead driving twin screws

FENELLA

Alongside its passenger ships, the Isle of Man Steam Packet Co. Ltd. had some small cargo ships, which carried much of the everyday requirements of the island, as well as cattle and cars. *Fenella* was the first motor ship the company owned, and this caused an unusual problem. At her berth in Douglas she was left high and dry between tides, meaning that her diesel generators could not be cooled by seawater. The solution was to use water from her ballast tanks.

Fenella had a long career serving the Isle of Man, and was sold only when its cargo trade was containerised. In 1973 she went to Greek owners to become *Vasso M* but in February 1977 she suffered a fire and became total loss.
Ailsa Shipbuilding Co. Ltd., Troon; 1951, 1,019gt, 223 feet
Seven-cylinder 2SCSA oil engine by British Polar Engines Ltd., Glasgow

LADY KILLARNEY

One of the reasons for creating Coast Lines in 1917 was to rationalise services between coastal ports, and inevitably this made some ships redundant. An imaginative solution to this problem was to run cruises in Scottish waters where spectacular scenery was guaranteed, even if the weather was not. Coast Lines first sent the steamer *Killarney* of 1893 cruising in 1931, and when they needed a replacement blended her name with that of the *Lady Connaught* to produce *Lady Killarney*.

This steamer had been built before the First World War as *Patriotic* for the Liverpool to Belfast service, but after she was replaced with a new motor ship in 1929 she was transferred to Dublin sailings, becoming first *Lady Leinster* and then *Lady Connaught*. After damage by a mine in the Mersey during 1940, she was reconstructed first as a cattle carrier and later as a hospital ship, and the latter left her ripe for conversion to a cruise ship. Reconstruction took place in 1952 but, sadly, this gave her only four years of new life. She was broken up in 1956, amidst much lamentation from her clientele - many of whom can be seen, well wrapped up, in the photograph below of her in final form.

Harland and Wolff Ltd., Belfast; 1912, 3,222gt, 325 feet
Two 4-cylinder triple expansion engines by Harland and Wolff Ltd., Belfast driving twin screws

INNISCARRA

Much of the Mersey's very important trade with Dublin was carried by the ships of the British and Irish Steam Packet Co. Ltd. This long-established company's acquisition by Coast Lines in 1919 made little difference to its regular passenger and cargo trades. However, Coast Lines had such an enormous fleet that there was much swapping of ships between companies in an effort to give each trade the most appropriate tonnage. For instance, the motor coaster *Inniscarra* had been built for Channel Island services as *Brittany Coast* in 1948 but was transferred to the Irish Sea in 1950.

The career of *Inniscarra* saw a major change in the ultimate ownership of British and Irish. In 1965, Coast Lines sold the company to the Irish Government, which was anxious to secure the future of one of Ireland's major shipping routes. *Inniscarra* herself was sold in 1970, made redundant by containerisation, and ran in the Mediterranean for a few years as *Elni* and later *Ria* until broken up in Italy during 1981.
Burntisland Shipbuilding Co. Ltd., Burntisland; 1948, 584gt, 177 feet
Five-cylinder 2SCSA oil engine by British Polar Engines Ltd., Glasgow

WELSH COAST

Coast Lines Ltd. was certainly Liverpool's - and possibly the world's - largest fleet of coastal ships, an achievement which owed much to the activities of Lord Kylsant. Something of a shipping megalomaniac, Kylsant steadily acquired companies towards the end of the First World War, his many coastal acquisitions coming under the banner of Coast Lines. When Kylsant's business empire fell apart around 1930, and he was sent to prison, the directors launched a successful rescue bid for Coast Lines.

Part of Kylsant's legacy was the widespread adoption of economical motor ships throughout his empire. Initially the new motor coasters for Coast Lines came from Dutch yards which were experienced in their production (see *Pascholl* on page 72), but soon Coast Lines' own yard, Ardrossan Dockyard Ltd., was producing economic little motor coasters like *Welsh Coast* of 1938.

After a 17-year career spent mainly on the Irish Sea, she moved to a Coast Lines subsidiary serving the Channel Islands to become *Guernsey Coast*. She seemed set for an equally long career sailing on the English Channel, but in August 1964 she was carrying tomatoes to Shoreham when she was sunk in collision with the *Catcher*, a Liberian-registered Liberty-type steamer.

Ardrossan Dockyard Ltd., Ardrossan; 1938, 646g, 209 feet
Six-cylinder 4SCSA oil engine by J.G. Kincaid and Co. Ltd., Greenock

CALEDONIAN COAST

Although the directors succeeded in pulling Coast Lines out of the rubble following the Kylsant crash, they were less successful in dealing with the relentless decline of coastal liner services in the years following the Second World War. That such services had been extensive and profitable was evidenced by ships such as *Caledonian Coast*, which was part of a service between Liverpool and London that called at Falmouth, Plymouth and Southampton, and which was much used in summer by passengers who wanted a short cruise. But she was taking five or six days to connect ports that were only 200 miles apart as the crow flies, and this laid the service wide open to competition from road haulage, especially once the M1 and M6 motorways opened. The service ceased in 1968, but then *Caledonian Coast* had a short Mediterranean holiday, working for Brocklebanks as *Makalla*. She was soon sold to Kuwaiti owners, who renamed her *Ahmadi Coast*. She was broken up at Cartagena, Spain in 1974.

Hall, Russell and Co. Ltd., Aberdeen; 1948, 1,265gt, 277 feet
Two 4-cylinder 2SCSA oil engines by British Polar Engines Ltd., Glasgow driving a single screw

ULSTER PRINCE

Photographs of the *Ulster Prince* are uncommon, as for most of the year she sailed in and out of Liverpool in darkness on the nightly passenger service to Belfast. This was one of Liverpool's most important short-sea services, and since the development of the steamship, the route was dominated by the Belfast Steamship Co. Ltd. After the company's takeover by Coast Lines in 1919 little changed until 1930, when three state-of-the-art motor ships were delivered, the first in the world built for cross-channel services. Sadly, only one survived the war, but *Leinster,* one of a pair of similar ships built for the Liverpool to Dublin service, was drafted in, taking the name *Ulster Prince*.

When a replacement arrived in 1966 and took her name, she was laid up as *Ulster Prince 1* until 1968 when a buyer was found. As *Adria* and later *Odysseus*, she became a cruise ship for Greek owners, although she can hardly be compared with the huge and hotel-like vessels that now dominate this market. At 40 years of age, her hull and engines were becoming worn out and increasingly expensive to maintain, and in July 1977 she was laid up at Glasgow. Two years later she was taken down the Clyde to Faslane to be broken up.

Harland and Wolff Ltd., Belfast; 1937, 4,303gt, 367 feet
Two oil engines 10-cylinder 4SCSA by Harland and Wolff Ltd., Belfast driving twin screws

ARDETTA

Just as ocean-going cargo liners have given way to container ships, their short-sea equivalents like the *Ardetta* have also been displaced. Her owners, the British and Continental Steamship Co. Ltd., operated regular services from Liverpool and Manchester to Antwerp and Rotterdam. Nowadays, the cargo they carried would go all the way on a lorry, using one of the nightly freight ferries from an east coast port or, increasingly, the Channel Tunnel. Changes like this help explain why the Mersey is now quiet compared with Basil Feilden's day, when British and Continental steamers would be in and out several times each week.

The Birkenhead-built *Ardetta* had a triple-expansion steam engine, which was obsolescent even when built, and she did well to survive in British service until 1965. As *Ocean Princess* she then had over a decade of further service, ending her days when broken up on Gadani Beach in Pakistan in May 1976.
Cammell, Laird and Co. Ltd., Birkenhead; 1949, 1,542gt, 289 feet
T. 3-cyl. by Cammell, Laird and Co. Ltd., Birkenhead

WOODLARK

The General Steam Navigation Co. Ltd. were, like British and Continental, operators of small cargo liners on near-continental and coastal services, although their routes were based largely on London and their ships were less familiar in Liverpool. It is a measure of how trade has changed that their fleet, which numbered almost fifty in 1950, had dwindled to half a dozen ships by the 1970s, and then disappeared into the fleet of its parent company, P. & O.

Woodlark was another steamer like *Ardetta;* cheap to build but not economic to run as the cost of fuel rose in post-war years. She survived in the General Steam fleet until 1954 when she was sold and renamed *Halcyon Med.* In 1956 she became *Asha* for Bombay owners, who were less concerned about running costs, and operated her until she was broken up in 1967.
Ailsa Shipbuilding Co. Ltd., Troon; 1928, 1,552gt, 240 feet
T. 3-cyl. by Ailsa Shipbuilding Co. Ltd., Troon

T.P. TILLING

Both photographs on this double-page spread show elderly steam coasters which were approaching the end of their days.

Built for John S. Monks and Co. Ltd., Liverpool, the *T.P. Tilling* was a typical steam coaster of a style which was fully developed by 1880. The raised quarter deck, between the bridge and engine room, was a feature which helped the coaster trim on an even keel when loaded. The engine was a simple triple-expansion steam engine, and she had a coal-fired Scotch boiler. Electric lighting was a luxury on such ships, and the crew - who were berthed right forward in the forecastle - had to make do with oil lamps.

Ships of her type would carry almost any bulk commodity around the Irish Sea: stone from North Wales quarries for building roads; grain transhipped from a visiting tramp to flour mills; china clay from Cornwall for onward despatch to the Potteries; but most frequently their cargo was coal from Liverpool or Garston to Belfast or Dublin. By the mid 1950s they were old and becoming uneconomic, *T.P. Tilling* going to breakers in Barrow-in-Furness during 1954.

J. Crichton and Co. Ltd., Saltney; 1920, 461gt, 142 feet
T. 3-cyl. by the Lytham Shipbuilding and Engineering Co. Ltd., Lytham

KYLEBROOK

It was unusual to see ships of *Kylebrook's* type on the Mersey, because these large colliers were designed for the coal trade from the Tyne and Wear down to London and the South Coast. Her original owners were based in Shoreham, and as *Algol* she would have rarely left the east and south coasts during her first 17 years.

Liverpool owners Monroe Brothers bought her in 1941, using her to bring steam coal from South Wales to fuel the Clarence Dock Power Station, whose chimneys can be seen in several Feilden photographs. At 35 years old, the ageing steamer was sold to breakers in Ghent during April 1959.

W. Dobson and Co., Newcastle-upon-Tyne; 1924, 1,578gt, 245 feet
T. 3-cyl. by North Eastern Marine Engineering Co. Ltd., Newcastle-upon-Tyne

PASCHOLL

The advent of Dutch motor vessels like *Pascholl* can partly explain the demise of steam coasters like *T.P. Tilling* (page 70). The Dutch made excellent profits during the First World War and, with money to invest, small shipowners built a new breed of motor ship. This was based on the hulls of their shallow-drafted sailing vessels with the addition of German diesel engines which had been developed to a high state of reliability for powering U-boats. These small Dutch coasters were economical and could go almost anywhere, undercutting the ponderous British steam coasters with their large appetites for coal.

Pascholl had a long and interesting life. She escaped the occupation of Holland in 1940 and, with a Royal Navy crew, was one of the little ships that helped rescue the British army from Dunkirk, taking off 695 servicemen. Re-engined by the British, she returned to Dutch owners after the war, and was later named *Volente*, which seems a bit ambitious given her speed of 7½ knots. In 1962 she went out to work in the Red Sea as *Mokha*, and was broken up at Aden in 1976.

N.V. Noord Nederlandsche Scheepswerven, Groningen, Holland; 1931, 257g, 122 feet

Four-cylinder 2SCSA oil engine by Crossley Brothers Ltd., Manchester, fitted 1944

JOZINA

One factor which helped make Dutch coasters like *Jozina* more economical than their British counterparts was that their captains were often their owners too. These captain-owners were coaster men from the towns of North Holland who, through hard work and favourable loans from Dutch banks and from their families, could buy and sail their own ship. Often, the ship was the family home, with the wife and children helping to run the ship, but not receiving wages. Money was also saved by minimising shoreside administration, although the captain-owners usually employed an agent to obtain their cargoes. In the case of *Jozina* this was the Van Uden agency in Rotterdam.

Jozina was sold in 1952 when only two years old, probably because of a good offer from the London and Rochester Trading Co. Ltd., who renamed her *Jubilence*. After a long, and one hopes profitable, career under the Red Ensign, she was sold to Greek owners in 1970 and renamed *Christoforos III*, then *Maneza, Agia Trias*, and finally *Agios Nikolaos*. But bestowing the name of a saint or a saintess, which Greek coaster owners often did, could not save *Agios Nikolaos* from the rigours of the sea, and she was wrecked on Fleves Island, not far from her home port of Piraeus, on 17th January 1986.

Scheepswerf 'Waterhuizen' J. Pattje, Waterhuizen, Holland; 1950, 500gt, 174 feet

Eight-cylinder 4SCSA oil engine by Gebr. Stork and Co. N.V., Hengelo, Holland

BENWOOD

If you can't beat 'em . . . Noting the success of the Dutch coaster, several British owners bought up these economical motor ships in the years after the Second World War. One such was Joseph Wilson, who had fostered an ambition to own ships since boyhood. In 1948 Wilson set up Mountwood Shipping Co. Ltd. which was named after the road in Birkenhead where he lived. *Benwood* was the second of three Dutch-built coasters which he was to own.

   Benwood had already had three names and at least as many owners. She was completed as the Dutch *Dr. Colijn*, becoming *Empire Crocus* in 1940 when war put her under the protection of the Ministry of War Transport. After the war she was renamed *Stainton* for Tees-side owners and became *Benwood* in 1951. Sold again in 1955, she spent her old age in Scandinavian hands, as *Monica, Mona* and finally *Scantic*. She cheated the breakers and was back in her old haunts on the Irish Sea in December 1964 when she foundered, although her crew of eight was rescued.

N.V. Noord-Nederlandsche Scheepswerven, Groningen, Holland; 1936, 341gt, 133 feet
Six-cylinder 4SCSA oil engine by Motoren Werke Mannheim A.G., vorm Benz and Co., Mannheim, Germany

SOMME

Today, many owners have their small coasters built with a low or retractable wheelhouse to allow them to work through the European inland waterway network. But this 'low air draught' is nothing new: in 1926 a Dutch owner, William Muller of Rotterdam, pioneered a service from Rotterdam to Paris with motor coasters which could pass beneath the Seine bridges, later extending his routes from Paris to the UK and Spain. For operations out of London, Muller found it convenient to have a local subsidiary and British-registered ships. Hence the motor coaster *Somme* was built, very unusually for a Dutch owner, in a British yard. She has low-height superstructure, funnel and bridge, with no bridge deck, and her masts could be folded on deck to clear bridges.

   After a creditable 27 years with one name and one owner, she had five of each in a dozen years after being sold: *Doxa, Eliva, Asopi, St. Patrick* and finally *Antonello*. She was broken up in Tunisia during 1989.

Henry Scarr Ltd., Hessle; 1950, 451gt, 161 feet
Six-cylinder 2SCSA oil engine by British Polar Engines Ltd., Glasgow

ALCHYMIST

F.T. Everard and Sons Ltd. began with Thames sailing barges and quickly progressed to being one of the largest British operators of motor coasters. Their fleet included both dry cargo and tanker tonnage and, given the density of the petrochemical industry on Merseyside, the tankers were - and remain - frequent visitors. Everards' coasters were usually distinguished by names of family members or names ending in -ity, but there were several exceptions, including *Alchymist*, which commemorated a name acquired with one of the company's first tankers.

Alchymist was another war standard type, of the *Empire Cadet* type, some of the most numerous coastal tankers built during the Second World War. Her original name was *Empire Orkney*, becoming *Alchymist* when bought and renamed by Everards in 1949. She traded round the coast until May 1969 when she sailed up the canal to Bruges in Belgium to be broken up.

A. and J. Inglis Ltd., Glasgow; 1945, 813gt, 193 feet
T. 3-cyl. by Aitchison, Blair Ltd., Glasgow

SAN SALVADOR

The Eagle Tanker Co. Ltd., owners of *San Salvador*, was the successor of a company formed in 1912 to bring Mexican oil to Europe. The company was a believer in large tankers, and some of the vessels completed for Eagle just before the First World War were then the largest in the world.

Eagle Oil tankers were managed by Shell from 1919, and the companies became ever closer, culminating in a complete takeover in 1959, after which *San Salvador* was effectively part of the Shell fleet. But although she painted up Shell's funnel she never acquired the name of a shell.

Her machinery was based on that of the wartime T2 tankers (see *Chemawa* on page 76), and comprised a turbine driving a dynamo to generate electricity to power an electric motor which turned the propellor. In contrast to the success of the T2s, *San Salvador's* arrangement did not prove satisfactory in service, and contributed to her early demise. She was scrapped in Holland in 1961, when barely 11 years old.

Furness Shipbuilding Co. Ltd., Haverton Hill-on-Tees; 1950, 10,802gt, 537 feet
Steam turbine driving electric motor by General Electric Co., Erith

OMALA

Tankers of various sizes have become an increasingly familiar sight on the Mersey, particularly since Shell chose to build a refinery on what were once lonely marshes on the banks of the Manchester Ship Canal. Stanlow is now the largest refinery in Britain and, with its associated petrochemical plants, this explains why tankers now dominate the traffic to the upper part of the Mersey.

Shell, a joint British and Dutch company, maintained a large fleet under both these flags and others. Here, Basil Feilden has recorded the Dutch-registered motor tanker *Omala* cautiously approaching Eastham Locks. In 1959, at 21 years - a good age for a tanker which is worked hard - *Omala* was delivered to shipbreakers at Blyth.

Cantieri Riuniti Dell'Adriatico, Trieste, Italy; 1938, 6,244gt, 446 feet
Six-cylinder 2SCSA Werkspoor oil engine by Cantieri Riuniti Dell'Adriatico, Trieste, Italy

NORRISIA

As one of the world's largest oil companies, Shell did not do things by halves, and from time to time it placed some massive orders for tankers. For instance, the *Norrisia* was just one of the 26 N class ships delivered from British yards between 1942 and 1946.

Some of the Ns built during the war were modified to became merchant aircraft carriers. They still had tanks for oil cargoes, but were fitted with flight decks so that one or two fighter aircraft could be carried to help protect their convoy.

In 1958 *Norrisia* became a storage hulk at Lulea, Sweden, but two years later she was broken up at La Spezia in Italy.

Harland and Wolff Ltd., Belfast; 1944, 8,246gt, 483 feet
Six-cylinder 4SCSA oil engines by Harland and Wolff Ltd., Belfast

VERENA

When *Verena* and her three sisters were delivered to Shell around 1950, they were the largest tankers built in the UK. Too big for contemporary diesels, they had steam turbines which could drive them along at 15 knots. The Vs had huge crews of 70; around three times the number that man today's equivalent, the very large crude carrier.

By the time *Verena* was broken up at Castellon in Spain during 1971, she had been dwarfed by the massive tankers which succeeded her.

Harland and Wolff Ltd., Belfast; 1950, 18,612gt, 643 feet
Two steam turbines by Harland and Wolff Ltd., Belfast driving a single screw

CHEMAWA

When the USA began its massive wartime expansion of its merchant fleet, it was very conscious of the need for tankers which were fast enough to keep up with and refuel its warships. It was planned to build these tankers with steam turbine machinery, but the necessary machine tools to cut the gears needed to transmit the turbine's power to a propellor were not available. Hence the ships were designed with turbines which drove a generator, the electrical power being fed to an electric motor which drove the screw.

Almost 500 of these T2 type tankers were built, and after the war most of the survivors were sold to commercial operators. *Chemawa*, unusually, kept her wartime name when acquired by a US company who registered her in Panama.

The T2 tankers were remarkable for the ship surgery which was carried out on them, with good bits of one ship being joined to good sections of others, or to newly-constructed sections. In June 1960 the engines and stern of *Chemawa* was joined to a new front part built by Blohm und Voss in Hamburg, and the resulting 'new' ship was named *Barbara Jane Conway*. This gave a useful extension of her life, and she served with the same owners until broken up in 1975.

Kaiser Company Inc., Swan Island Yard, Portland, Oregon, USA; 1945, 10,448gt, 504 feet
Steam turbine driving electric motor by General Electric Co., Lynn, Massachusetts, USA

OLJAREN

When Basil Feilden photographed the tanker *Oljaren* her after end showed the scars of an encounter with the Muckle Skerry Rocks in the Pentland Firth during April 1951. She was lucky to survive: abandoned by her crew on 14th April, a salvage company managed to refloat her on 30th April, and she was sent to the Mersey for repair.

The World Ship Society's journal 'Marine News' for July 1951 carries an eye-witness account of her in Brocklebank Dry Dock. It speaks of a rent in *Oljaren's* hull from the keel to the upper deck, which was itself buckled, and through which her tanks were visible. The plating around the engine room was ripped so that her machinery could be seen from the dockside. Although expected to be repaired in Birkenhead, *Oljaren* was actually sent to Bremerhaven to have the work done.

After this adventure, *Oljaren* was renamed *Kalmia* although still owned by Rederi A/B Transatlantic of Sweden. In 1958 she was sold and as *Ornak* saw out her days in Polish ownership, being broken up in the repair yard at Gdansk during 1966.
A/B Götaverken, Gothenburg, Sweden; 1947, 8,337gt, 484 feet
Six-cylinder 2SCSA oil engine by A/B Götaverken, Gothenburg, Sweden

ISHAV

Seeking to expand their operations between the wars, Scandinavian shipowners correctly identified the petroleum trade as a potential growth area. In the 1930s, whilst UK owners were still putting their faith largely in dry cargo tonnage, the Scandinavians invested heavily in tankers. Hence, in the 1950s, most of the 'independent' tankers which the oil companies relied on to supplement their own fleets flew the flag of Denmark, Sweden or - in the case of *Ishav* - Norway.

Ishav worked for original owner Per Lodding until 1964 when she hoisted the Liberian flag as *Maribruna* for a company in the Chandris group. She was scrapped in Taiwan during 1969.
Kockums A/B, Malmo, Sweden; 1951, 10,451gt, 533 feet
Eight-cylinder 2SCDA oil engine by Kockums A/B, Malmo, Sweden

SOUTHERN HARVESTER

It is hard now to condone the gruesome and wasteful business of whaling but, in the years immediately after the Second World War, whale oil was in demand and whale meat was still considered - at least by those who did not have to eat it - as an important contribution to the British diet. Factory ships like the *Southern Harvester* would leave the northern hemisphere each autumn for the whaling grounds off the Antarctic. Their accompanying catchers would harpoon whales, which were drawn up the factory ship's stern ramp to extract their oil and meat. Each spring the factory ships would return, often to the Mersey where their oil would be unloaded, before going into summer lay-up in a Norwegian fjord.

The last British company to take part in whaling was the South Georgia Co. Ltd., a subsidiary of Christian Salvesen of Leith. *Southern Harvester* was their last whale factory ship, withdrawn from whaling in 1963 when she was sold, together with her quota of whales, to the Japanese. The buyers were more interested in her quota than the ship itself, and she remained laid up at Tonsberg. She had a period as a floating workshop from 1968 until 1971, when she was broken up at Santander in Spain.
Furness Shipbuilding Co. Ltd., Haverton Hill-on-Tees; 1946, 15,364gt, 540 feet
T. 6-cyl. by North Eastern Marine Engineering Co. Ltd., Wallsend-on-Tyne

BALAENA

Balaena, a contemporary of *Southern Harvester*, was a bigger, better-equipped and in many ways more successful factory ship. The large structure just aft of her funnels is a hangar to house the aircraft she carried to spot whales. Her owners were Hector Whaling Ltd., a British company with a strong Norwegian shareholding.

With British, Norwegian, Dutch, Russian, Japanese, Argentinean and Panamanian whaling expeditions each year, and with catching methods getting more sophisticated, the industry was signing a death warrant, not only for thousands of whales, but also for itself. In the late 1950s, expeditions were having difficulty finding the numbers of whales allowed under the unrealistically large quotas allocated by the International Whaling Commission. In 1960 *Balaena* was sold to the Japanese, who had more of a taste for whale meat than the British, and she became *Kyokuyo Maru No. 3*. Although not scrapped until 1978, it seems unlikely that she would have found enough whales to process in later years, and was probably laid up.

The stern ramp, up which the whales' carcasses were pulled for processing, is clearly seen as *Balaena* enters Gladstone Dock.
Harland and Wolff Ltd., Belfast; 1946, 15,715gt, 555 feet
T. 6-cyl. by Harland and Wolff Ltd., Belfast driving twin screws

PIONIER

Basil Feilden would have had few chances to photograph visitors from Germany in the decade following the war. The country was desperately short of tonnage, as most modern and relatively undamaged German ships had been taken and shared out amongst the Allies in 1945. They were left with a few veterans, like *Pionier* which is by far the oldest ship in this book. Notice also the number 804, to show that *Pionier* was licensed to trade by the Allied Control Commission which regulated German shipping.

With timber being relatively light, a ship would not be down to her marks with the amount that could be stowed in its holds. Additional timber was therefore often carried as a deck cargo. However, timber on deck

tended to become waterlogged in bad weather, explaining the obvious list in this photograph.

Very early in 1953, her owner Richard Homuth sold *Pionier* to another German company who planned to trade her in the Red Sea. Unfortunately, the ship stranded on the Dutch coast at the end of January, and at 80 years old was fit only to be taken back to Germany for demolition.

Reiherstieg Schiffswerf und Maschine Fabriek, Hamburg, Germany; 1873, 417gt, 160 feet
C. 2-cyl. by Reiherstieg Schiffswerf und Maschine Fabriek, Hamburg, Germany

Index of ships

Names in CAPITALS are those carried by ships in photographs. Names in upper and lower case are other names carried.